The Reset

Bob,

May THE RESET give you a fresh appreciation for how much God loves you and wants a deep, intimate daily walk with you.

"Greater is He..."
1 John 4:4

David Stevens

The Reset

Reclaiming The Life You Should
Be Living In 28 Days

DAVID STEVENS

WESTBOW
P R E S S
A DIVISION OF THOMAS NELSON

WestBow Press books may be ordered through booksellers or by contacting:

WestBow Press
A Division of Thomas Nelson
1663 Liberty Drive
Bloomington, IN 47403
www.westbowpress.com
1-(866) 928-1240

ISBN: 978-1-4497-2977-6 (sc)
ISBN: 978-1-4497-2978-3 (hc)
ISBN: 978-1-4497-2976-9 (e)

Library of Congress Control Number: 2011918904

Printed in the United States of America

WestBow Press rev. date: 11/02/2011

To the memory of my father-in-law,

Rev. Sidney V. Murphy,

whose legacy of faithfully reading his Bible,

his dedicated prayer life, and his daily walk with God,

will never be forgotten by

his wife of sixty-eight years,

Ora Brandon Murphy,

his three children,

Sidney Vaughn Murphy,

Pamela Murphy Stevens,

Mark Norman Murphy,

and all of his grandchildren and great-grandchildren.

CONTENTS

FOREWORD

Our dad finally wrote the book he was destined to write. In *The Reset*, he presents the ideas and concepts that he instilled in us growing up. It is even better to finally have this in book form, not only for us to review as adults, but also because this life-transforming, 28-day journey can now be shared with many others. It is unlike most other books that promise to deliver change to your life; not only is it practical and engaging, but it works! Furthermore, it will stick with you for the rest of your life.

He clearly shows readers how to reclaim the life that they should be living by learning and internalizing his seven *Resets*. He calls the fourth *Reset* the "Ultimate Reset," and you will not want to miss that one! By following the simple things that he asks you to do on this 28-day journey, you will be able to experience a fresh start in your life and get what we have absorbed into our personal lives over the past twenty-six years.

As we now look back, we appreciate and realize the tremendous impact that our dad has not only made in our lives, but also in the lives of so many others during his years as a pastor and a children's pastor. *The Reset* creatively weaves together many personal life experiences from our family, along with other illustrations from everyday life. You will soon be tapping into an overflowing source of hope and experiencing a genuine transformation that will change your life forever. We know that our dad has poured his life into this book in order that everyone who reads and applies his seven *Resets* will never ever again have to feel that their lives are hopeless. Read this book, and you will discover that **"no matter what start you had, you can now have a great finish!"**

Jonathan and Jeremiah Stevens

Day 1

Introduction:
"One Shining Moment,
You Reached for the Sky!"

"That one shining moment, you reached for the sky!
One shining moment, you were willing to try!"[1]

—from "One Shining Moment" by David Barrett

I absolutely love that famous song, which plays during the highlight video of the just-completed final Monday night game of the men's college basketball tournament! Whether my favorite team has won or lost, my family knows that the volume is going way up on the sound system in my house when the highlight video starts playing. In that "One Shining Moment" video, every possible human emotion and reaction to the tournament's games is on full display in the faces of the players, coaches, fans, cheerleaders, and even the various team mascots.

Sports enthusiasts know that this three-week period has forever been marked on annual calendars as "March Madness." Each year, the college basketball season culminates when the tournament bracket positions sixty-plus teams in head-to-head competition, giving their utmost to be the national champion that year. Every team but one will ultimately lose their final game of the season. The one team left standing at the end of the "Road to the Final Four" proudly accepts and lifts high above their heads the coveted trophy of the national championship. That is when the synchronized music video starts, and we get the spine-chilling latest version of the epic "One Shining Moment!"

In two or three fast-paced minutes, we see everything from spectacular plays and critical turnovers to buzzer-beating winning shots and the oh-so-close desperation of last-second misses. Some players are leaping into human piles of joy and celebration, while others are crumbling to the floor in exhaustion and disappointment. There are hands held high in jubilant victory, and then there are faces buried in hands, hiding tears of defeat. The cameras often zoom in to catch and freeze-frame those split-second, raw, and spontaneous facial expressions revealing the deepest inner emotions that emerge from valiant attempts to survive and play just one more game.

For each player, it all comes down to the all-out effort given and to the pursuit of doing one's best, win or lose. It is all on the line! If they have given it their very best, then they have not let themselves or their teammates down. Only one team and one "Most Outstanding Player" will take home the top trophies. However, in reality, every player and every coach who participates in the "big dance" can finish his season feeling like a winner. It is rewarding enough just to make it into the tournament and to have given it your best shot. It is their "one shining moment!"

That Is What We All Want out of Life!

For all of us, life is a journey, and we really want to give it our best shot every day! Even though we can only see in part where our daily journey is taking us and what the cumulative outcomes will be, we would like to feel good about our efforts and ourselves at the end of each day. Perhaps a highlight video each evening showing our "one shining moment" for that day would help us all sleep a little better and be more excited about facing tomorrow's agenda and portion of the journey. Yet deep inside, most of us end our days yearning for a different routine with a sense of purpose and meaning, at least something that would inspire the best out of us each day. If only we could first escape the self-inflicted busy rat race that we live in, then we could go for it and try to reclaim the elusive life that we should be living and that we are currently missing on most days. In your life's journey so far, do you feel that on most days you are living up to the full potential of your life? On the other hand, do you often lack a sense of real direction and purpose in your life?

The Journey We Call Life Has Choices

Being on a journey can involve many different stages over an extended period. This is especially true of our lives. Each one of us starts life with an unknown number of years on this earth. We all have a specific beginning and an eventual end to our lives. In between those two reference points or dates is our own personal journey that we call life. As someone has wisely noted, it is the little dash on our tombstone, situated between our birth date and our death date, which will ultimately sum up our lives. If it could talk, it would tell the stories of our earthly journeys, the good and the bad, the pretty and the ugly.

Since we do have choices in life, how then should we choose to live? There has always been one very fulfilling way to live this life. God originally programmed the first human couple with this life, but of course they chose to rebel and sin against God, and the human race has pretty well messed it up ever since. God even sent—in the flesh—his very own son, Jesus, to redeem this way of life humanity had lost. However, many people down through the ages have opted out of God's way and instead have chosen to pursue life their own ways and on their own terms. To some degree, that has been the tempting dilemma for us all! Simply stated, we would rather chart our own journeys in life.

The biblical account of the prodigal son (Luke 15) is a good example of what all of us do at various points of our journeys. If you read that story again, you'll see how the choices that the prodigal son made led to terrible consequences in his life. The Bible is consistently clear that in this life we will have times of difficulty simply because we live in a fallen and sinful world. However, we only magnify our difficulties when we choose to live differently than the way God intended for us to live. The pain and scars that you and I inflict on others and ourselves by deliberately going against God's way can also be passed on to future generations in our family tree. The good news is that we can always choose to change our ways of thinking and our ways of living. We can choose to do a *reset* and allow a restoration process to put us back on the right course for the rest of our life's journey! In fact, no matter how badly you think that you may have messed up your life, this *Reset* can even work for you!

You Can *Reset* Your Life If That Is What You Really Want!

This book, called *The Reset,* presents you with a 28-day journey to change your life by changing the way you think. We will use the analogy of a "reset button" to help us imagine the possibility of recapturing the kind of day-to-day life that we would all like to experience and enjoy.

Perhaps you know the feeling that you have experienced when your computer freezes up on you, or without cause, it totally changes the entire configuration on your screen. You have no clue how to fix the problem, and there are probably no computer geeks living in your household to help you. The only hope you have is that maybe there is an option of somehow going back to an original default setting. If you have a problem with some other kind of high tech device, you may even have the possibility of pushing a reset button that will return everything back to the original settings and give you and your sanity a fresh start.

The Reset will gradually enable you to activate and implement a 28-day *reset* of your thinking about yourself and about the one who originally put you together. You will soon be enjoying a fresh start to your life with a completely restored perspective. Soon you will know what real joy, strength, and inner peace is like. We live in rapidly changing and difficult times. So why not give yourself and your thinking a *reset,* and discover how to live your life with new meaning and purpose, and go out into the world every day with an overflowing confident hope, despite the daily challenges that you will face? Start now by reading this biblical verse, and believe that a life-changing *reset* is possible for you in the next 28 days!

"Let God transform *you* into a new person by changing the way *you* think" (Romans 12:2 NLV, emphasis added).

Congratulations! This journey will definitely help you start pursuing your own daily "shining moments" that you have probably been missing. I welcome you to this exciting 28-day *reset* journey!

Review

1. Read *Romans 12:2* slowly to yourself several times, focusing your thoughts on each word.
2. Now *substitute your name* where the word *you* is used.
3. Commit yourself now to reading just *one chapter a day for the next 28 days.* Tomorrow, we will begin with your own fresh start!

Today's Prayer

Dear God,

If you really can help me transform my life, I could use your help at this time. I feel like I am missing something in the way I am currently living. I am not sure what it is, but I am willing to try this 28-day book to *reset* my life. Help me to be patient with myself and to believe that positive changes can come to me. O God, renew my hope today for a fresh start and begin restoring my purpose and meaning in life. Amen.

Day 2

A Fresh Start Would Be Nice

Let's face a quick dose of reality. First, everyday life can—at times—be excruciatingly tough on us! On top of that, everything that is going on in the world around us and in our personal lives can make us feel very disoriented and confused. Today, there is a growing sense for many people in all stages of life of a deep inner unrest about who we are and where we are going. We feel like we are rapidly losing control over many things in our lives that in years past seemed to be more steady and reliable.

In just the last few years, anxiety levels for most people have risen dramatically because of the daily threat of worldwide terrorism. Add to that the uncertain and downright scary economic fluctuations that have affected so many homes and families. There is a growing distrust in government and in our elected political figures. Over the years, there have been some highly visible scandals within religious circles. Add to this short list the many highly emotionally charged challenges taking place in the public debate and in our courts, which threaten to unravel and undo many of our long-held traditional cultural values.

It can sometimes feel overwhelming, almost as if we have found ourselves on the last over-crowded lifeboat and just dropped and slammed into a raging sea at night. We soon discover that we have no food or supplies, no navigational or communications ability, and no sense of our whereabouts. We don't even have an anchor to hold our little lifeboats steady until a possible life-saving rescue can arrive.

Furthermore, the reality of everyday, normal life tells us that if we are not in some kind of personal "pickle" right now, watch out, one is coming our way soon. Families and businesses are facing tremendous struggles and pressures to stay together and survive and to make ends meet financially. Yet, the twenty-first century is not the first generation of people to face troubling days. History is full of turbulent and volatile periods going all the way back to biblical times. The cycles have been repeating themselves throughout human history. Even the Bible is very honest in telling us that we will always be facing trials and sufferings in this life.

On a personal level, the most difficult experiences for us as individuals to navigate through are usually the ones involving either personal failures of our own doing, the cold and heartless personal rejections of others (such as parents, spouses, close friends, or co-workers), or from our own deep, personal disillusionments of how life is turning out for us.

When life throws those big, ugly curves at us, we all desperately need something that will steady our knees and strengthen our spines to help us survive victoriously through each difficulty. While the saying, "it is always too early to give up" is catchy to say, it is always easier said than done!

Left alone to our own limited and frail human resources, we often try to muscle up a variety of lone-ranger efforts to fix our problems and dig out on our own. The fixes are often only superficial and temporary, like putting duct tape around a broken water pipe. It sure would be better if we could just stumble upon a reset button hidden somewhere in the closet of our lives that we could push and go back to a better place and time and start all over.

Commonly Failed Approaches

Most of the time, we eventually approach our failures and disappointments in life by saying to ourselves (which is self-talk) something like the following: *I always make a mess of my life, but I am really going to change this time. I can do better than that, and I won't make the same mistakes again!*

On the other hand, if you have ever been prone to try a spring-cleaning approach, you probably vowed to start over and perform a list of certain personal things better, in other words, to clean up your act. You reasoned that if your performance in a few key areas improved, then life would most definitely start dealing you a better hand to work with.

If you went even further, you probably reverted to a common but misunderstood spiritual approach. If you could just diligently do more religious things to earn God's approval and passing grade, then He would begin blessing you and stop all the negative things from happening to you. If you are by yourself right now reading this book, go ahead and raise your hand to acknowledge that you have tried this approach before. Even if someone else might see you raising your hand, do it anyway. Just smile and tell them they have done it too. It will just make them wonder!

A Better Way to Accomplish a Genuine *Reset*

The rest of this book will show you a real way that you can experience a life changing *reset*, even if you have personally messed up big time. By the way, you are in the majority crowd on that note: "For everyone has sinned; we all fall short of God's glorious standard." From that Scripture found in Romans 3:23, *fall short* can mean, "messed up big time." On our own, we all miss the mark of God's standard rather routinely.

If the possibility of a fresh start or a second chance has aroused your curiosity, then read on. Just imagine the following and be honest. If I placed before you now a big, red, life-reset button, which guaranteed you a fresh start, would it be tempting for you to just push it and give it a try? Well, we both know that there is no such red magical button, or I would be out today selling a lot of big, red buttons rather than sharing this 28-day book journey with you.

Therefore, I ask you to stay with me each day and to do the simple things that I encourage you to do. Then you will begin to discover and experience for yourself life that is full of "shining moments" and one that restores purpose and meaning and hope to each day that you live.

The Mind and Heart Work Together for Good or Bad

Our Creator put us together in a way that has our minds and our hearts (who we are at the deepest core level) wired and working together. In essence, we ultimately believe, become, and act out what we think about the most. Even what other people have said to us during every stage of our lives can affect us if we accept and internalize their messages.

Our minds act like a computer. They receive, store, and process all the input that we allow them to receive. Simply put, what we think or say about ourselves or what others say about us gets into our internal storage and ultimately works either for us or against us. Our responsibility in this process is to be like a faithful and dependable gatekeeper to our minds, letting in the positive, healthy, empowering, and faith-filled thoughts, while turning away the negative, destructive, defeating, and doubting thoughts.

A simple formula for how this process works would be: *Input* (the messages we receive and embrace from God, self, others, or cultural sources) form our *core beliefs*. Our core beliefs then determine our *attitudes*, which in turn affect our *feelings*. Our feelings ultimately play out in our daily personal behaviors or our *actions*. Our behaviors or actions then collectively bring about the *results* or outcomes of our daily lives. The progression then looks like this:

INPUT—CORE BELIEFS—ATTITUDES—FEELINGS—ACTIONS—RESULTS[1]

Input in the above formula is what we will refer to in this 28-day journey as our *reset self-talk statements*. Studies have shown that the impact of the cumulative layers of negative self-talk (input) that we have received, accepted, and stored from what others said to us when we were growing up as children is staggering. The comments may have not seemed like such a big deal when we first heard them, but oh, how they can still surface, hurt us, and paralyze us in some critical areas of our lives.

Furthermore, much of our own input or personal self-talk can and does continue to be somewhat negative and self-defeating, unless we recognize and understand the process. Then we must begin to change the patterns of how we think and what we say to ourselves.

As you continue this journey, I hope you will commit to allowing God to help you change or alter the input of your thinking and to become faithful gatekeepers of your thoughts and self-talk. In fact, our launching pad verse for this exciting journey will be Romans 12:2:

"Let God transform you into a new person by changing the way you think."

You will quickly discover that changing some of your thoughts is not easy at first. Old negative thought patterns can have deep personal and extensively stubborn family roots. We will start tomorrow by gradually unfolding the first of seven biblically inspired new self-talk *Reset* statements that you will write out, take with you, and commit to memory. Every day you will review and use these *Reset* statements and the supporting biblical verses to transform and change your thinking.

At the beginning of this 28-day journey, you will also realize that many old thoughts, perhaps imbedded for a long time, will stubbornly resist any new thoughts coming into the neighborhood. That is quite normal. But understand that it is about time that they need to be forced to move out anyway, and that you will have to just let them go. We will be quickly replacing them anyway with much better thoughts.

Tomorrow, I will share how a greeting card and a simple impression from God began to shape in my own mind the first of our seven self-talk statements that will become the focus of your own personal *reset* journey. For now, let me tell you how excited I am to have you reading this 28-day *reset* book! Soon, you will have an overflowing, confident hope walking out the door with you every day. You will live your life reaching for the sky and giving it your best shot without any regrets. Then, one last day, all of your "shining moments" will define the "dash" in your life.

Today's Important Action Step

Get yourself at least seven index cards to start using for your self-talk *Reset* statements. You will be writing the statements on the *front* of the index cards and then using the *back* of the cards to write out the supportive biblical verses. You may use any size card, but it may be better to get a larger size card to have plenty of room for our statements and verses.

As you go through the rest of this first day, allow Romans 12:2 to move in and make a home in your mind and heart. Write the verse out on the top one-half of the back of your first index card and take it with you. Read it to yourself and when possible, say it aloud to yourself until you begin to memorize it.

As a note, for this journey I have chosen to use exclusively the New Living Translation (NLT) of the Bible. Let me encourage you to stick with this version for the supportive verses, even if you want to compare them with other versions of the Bible that you may have.

While you are memorizing Romans 12:2 throughout the day, try placing a focus or emphasis on different words or phrases each time you repeat the verse. Accept each word and phrase at its face value because they are inspired and empowered as the authoritative words of Scripture. God is willing to do his part, so as the verse says, let him begin doing it in your life today!

"Let God transform you into a new person by changing the way you think" Romans 12:2.

Review

Read Romans 12:2 aloud five times, and then try to fill in the blanks below.

"____ God transform you into a ____ _____ by _____ the way you _____"
Romans ___ : ___.

Today's Prayer

Dear God,

I am excited to begin learning more about *The Reset*. I could certainly use some fresh thinking and a fresh start in my life right now. I simply ask you today to give me some hope that my life can be renewed or restored in positive ways. Take all my past and present circumstances, my disillusionments and my brokenness, and help me to begin to see that you have a way of making things turn out for good. Today, I am willing to begin hoping for that fresh start from you. Amen.

RESET #1

Day 3

You Are on God's Mind Again Today

Words are powerful forces in our lives for either good or bad. In the earthly realm, from the day we are born, we are constantly hearing what others are saying about us. This starts the day we are born, and it continues throughout our developmental years. Before we are old enough to discern the validity and the truth or lies of these words, we internalize many of them, not knowing their full impact and the consequences on our behaviors and our lives.

There are also words spoken about us in the spiritual realm. There are the words of God, and then there are the words of Satan. God speaks blessings toward us while our archenemy speaks curses. They are waging a war over our very lives. Whom we listen to and what we believe about what they have said will ultimately determine the outcome of our lives. For now, just keep in mind that the words of others affect our lives greatly. The good news is that we can choose which words we want to hear and believe!

Today, I want to share with you how the encouraging words of others have influenced my life and what inspired me to write this book.

Several times in my life, I have received a note or a card in the mail that just made my day. I am not talking about the expected annual birthday card or two that may find their way into my mailbox. No, it has been those rare and unexpected cards of encouragement and cheer that come when the "bottom has just fallen out" or when the circumstances that I was facing seemed at the time to be utterly hopeless. My Aunt Theresa sent me one of those encouragement cards many years ago that I saved and still cherish today. Thank you, Aunt Theresa! It is during those times that we discover who our closest friends and supporters really are.

Most of the senders of those cards rarely knew the full impact that their cards had on my life, even though I usually expressed my gratitude for being the recipient of their thoughtfulness. By the way, that word, *impact,* is a perfect description of how powerful and life changing just a few thoughtful handwritten words in a card can be.

Even though their words may have been few in number, I knew that someone was thinking of me, and that alone renewed my hope. Someone cared, and they cared enough to reach out to me. Now that is a true friend indeed!

The Power of a Few Sincere Words

Zig Ziglar wrote these words in a book on parenting, "You never know when a moment and a few sincere words can have an impact on a life."[1] To impact something has the connotation of one body forcefully colliding with another body, resulting forever in a new course or destiny for each of them. That phrase jumped off the page when I first read it over twenty years ago and, for some reason, it super-glued itself into my brain. At that time, it gave me a new appreciation for my awesome new task and privilege of being a brand-new father. It also helped launch a ministry desire to become a children's pastor. I wanted not only to impact children's lives personally, but also to help teach parents and other influential adults how to raise positive kids in a negative world. Our stated children's ministry vision was "to help families get their kids on God's team and become real winners in life." I became convinced that in human interactions, the impact or influence of spoken or written words to children or someone else could be very positive or very negative. They can contain either blessings or curses that affect every facet of a person's life.

"Just Thought I Would Say Hello, for You Were on My Mind"

Even though our culture today uses many other means besides the US Postal Service to deliver thoughts of encouragement, such as e-mail, texting, and tweeting, let me share how a simple traditional snail-mail card of encouragement helped *reset* my thoughts many years ago.

This book, called *The Reset*, had its conceiving moment one day when I was looking for the perfect encouragement card to send to a friend of mine who was going through some personal tragedies. A simple and appropriate card quickly caught my attention in the store. On the outside was a simple but beautiful golden sunset picture, along with these short words, "Thinking of You." But it was the inside inscription that impacted me and started resetting my thoughts and ultimately gave me the impulse to write this book. When I opened the card and read the words, "Just thought I would say hello, for you were on my mind," it was as if God was trying to say those words directly to me! It just so happened that, at that time, I was going through a personal trial of my own. I could not explain it, but I could just sense that God wanted to teach me something in a deeper way than I had ever understood before. I bought two of the cards and sent one card to my friend with a short handwritten note of encouragement. I kept the other card for myself, just to dwell on. I wanted to discover what God was trying to show me.

I tucked that extra card into my Bible where it stayed for a few days until my daily reading found me one day focusing on Psalm 139:17. "How precious are your thoughts about me, O God. They cannot be numbered." Then it started coming together, and one thought would lead to another. I still get goose bumps thinking about how it all unfolded and how God leads us when we are available and open to His leading.

Later that same day, when I opened my e-mail to check my messages, the familiar computerized voice proclaimed, "You've got mail!" That prompted my mind's usually slow processor to pick up speed, and soon I was back to thinking about that card again. "Thinking of You . . . Just thought I would say hello, for you were on my mind." Then I quickly made the connection back to the verse in Psalm 139 again. "How precious are your thoughts about me, O God. They cannot be numbered."

I was definitely having a God-moment. He was finally getting through to me. Then suddenly, another connecting "ah-ha" thing happened. My iPod, which was playing quietly into the room's sound system, changed to a new song. Read and contemplate for a moment these words from a contemporary Christian song, entitled "He Knows My Name."

> *I have a Father. He calls me His own. He'll never*
> *leave me. No matter where I go. He knows my name.*

Wow! I had been a believer since I was a young boy, but like most people, I needed a fresh reminder of just how much God thinks about me individually. Maybe you too have known about God's love in the past, but today you are just going through the routine motions of living and going to church. Perhaps you have heard about His love but have never been told how you can personally have a relationship with Him. Maybe you are not even going to church now or never have gone. Church has turned you off and bored you for one reason or another. It is quite possible that you have been around people or family members who claim to know about God's love, but what you observed in their lives didn't convince you that you needed what they had. It is sad to say, but that happens a lot.

That same evening while standing outside on a clear, crisp night and contemplating the stars overhead, I began to imagine God actually sending me a card that read what my card had said. "Thinking of you . . . Just thought I would say hello, for you were on my mind." Suddenly, tears welled up in my eyes, for it dawned on me that God actually does that. It may not arrive in my physical mailbox in a stamped envelope or in my e-mail inbox, but God does send me His caring thoughts through the Bible, through prayer, and through inspired songs like the one I quoted. He does know me! He knows my name. He cares about me. Why would He not? He made me!

You and I are on God's mind today and every day. David, the Psalmist, discovered this truth and we too can claim his declared promise. "How precious are your thoughts about me, O God. They cannot be numbered."

You Too Can Begin Your *Reset* Journey Right Now!

So that's how my simple *reset* journey got started, and I hope you will start yours today. I invite you to begin right here and simply dwell on and memorize our first *Reset* self-talk statement. This is just the first of seven *Reset* statements that we will learn together, so take the time now and write it out word-for-word on an index card. Then start saying it over and over again to yourself until you have absorbed the thought and actually begin to memorize it.

Learn one sentence at a time. As you repeat it aloud to yourself, again try adding emphasis to different words. Focus your thoughts each time on how that emphasized word or phrase adds a unique meaning to the whole sentence. Tomorrow, we will share with you how and why this daily new self-talk is so important for your *reset* journey.

Here is *Reset* #1.

I am on God's mind again today.

I really do matter to God, and He is always
thinking precious thoughts about me.

"Let God transform you into a new person
by changing the way you think" Romans 12:2.

"How precious are your thoughts about me, O God.
They cannot be numbered" Psalm 139:17.

Review

On the front of your first index card, write out *Reset* #1, word-for-word. Leave a little space between the two sentences and a little space at the bottom for some additions tomorrow. Now for review, see if you can fill in the blanks of our supportive verses.

"_____ God transform _____ into a new _____
by _____ the way you _____" Romans ___:2.

"How precious are your _____ _____ ___, O God.
They cannot be numbered" Psalm 139:_____.

Today's Prayer

Dear heavenly Father,

I am so glad that you personally know my name. I never really thought that much about how you are constantly thinking about me. I am really on your mind, and you want me to know how important my life is to you. To now know that and just think about it overwhelms me. My hope for a fresh start, a *reset* of my life, is getting stronger. Please take into account all that is going on in my life today. Some of it I just don't understand, so please send me a touch of encouragement from heaven. I am glad that I really matter to you. Amen.

Day 4

Changing How You See Yourself

I am so glad that you have started this *reset* journey. You have probably discovered that ongoing difficulties will always be a part of your life in this world. In these 28 days, you are going to see how your daily thoughts and attitudes can help you to not only simply survive your trials and setbacks, but also how they can enable you to finally enjoy and live out the life and destiny that God wants for you. Life will take on a completely new meaning when you discover that God wants you to see yourself as He sees you.

Today's topic is crucial. You must get it today, or the rest of our 28-day journey will not change a thing about your life. Embrace and receive this concept, and you will begin to see not only dramatic changes in the way you think, but you will also be on your way to your own personal *reset*.

Remember from yesterday that *you are on God's mind again today.* Whether the events in your life are good or not so good today, He does know your name, and you must truly believe that He has only precious thoughts about you, no matter what you have ever done. He declares this in many places in the pages of the Bible. God loves you deeply and cares about the painful hurts that you will go through in this sin-filled world.

That leads us to this next thought: not every bad thing that happens to you is your fault. Many times, you and I reap the natural consequences of our own poor decisions and actions. These are usually obvious to us. But often we will suffer through earthly trials because of the actions or behaviors of other people. Sinfulness in this world and the sinful actions of others will often wreak havoc in our lives personally. We will then make such comments as, "Life is not fair," or "Why should I have to pay the price for what they did to me?"

Have you ever said anything like that? Of course you have, and so have I. We have all suffered unjustly for the sinful actions of someone else. But we also suffer the good and bad consequences of our own actions. This will always be the case and will never change. It is the universal and biblical law of sowing and reaping.

Many people today also suffer from a faulty-thought disease, commonly called "victimitis." To a degree, all of us have had this disease at some time. Many studies have shown for instance that while we were growing up as children, most of us heard and received far more negative responses from the adults in our lives than we did positive ones. "Stop that!" "Don't you dare do it." "You can't go there." "You will never grow up!" I am sure that most of us can remember other negative comments that we received growing up as children.

Very few parents seem able to master the delicate art of balancing authoritative discipline with authentic unconditional love. Many times we as children needed to be told *no* for our own good, but in our busy culture, I agree with Zig Ziglar that we could do much better by raising positive kids in a negative world. Perhaps you were raised like many others in more of a negative environment, but if you were, you cannot allow yourself to be forever stuck in a victim mentality and living in permanent defeat.

The result of this onslaught of negative thinking (or mental programming), learned from either our childhoods or from our cultures, is that it becomes so easy to acquire and implement a destructive thought process that literally undermines our ability to live the lives that God wants for us to enjoy. Think about it. How many times have you ever said or just thought something like the following (you can fill in the blanks)?

"I just can't _____."

"I never seem to have _____."

"I'm just not any good at _____."

"If only I were just _____."

"I mess up every time I _____."

You could probably add a few more statements of your own. These are typical examples of *negative self-talk*. Without thinking, we often say or think statements like this out of habit. Unless we become aware of it and make a conscious effort to break this self-sabotaging habit and literally start changing how we think, we continue to make it unlikely that we will ever reclaim the lives that we should be living.

The point is that our minds and our hearts work incredibly together, but again for either good or bad. It is like the old example of a good computer system that works efficiently. Good input always equals good output. On the other hand, trash in means trash out.

A major thrust of this 28-day *reset* is to learn to change the way we think and, with God's help, to empower ourselves to become more of what He originally intended for us to be like.

A Baby Tiger Who Had a Wrong Perception of Himself[1]

One of my favorite stories is about a little baby tiger that got separated and lost and somehow mixed up with a herd of goats. This baby tiger mistakenly began to think that he was a little baby goat and suddenly began to nibble at the green grass and make little bleating-like sounds similar to all the other goats, even as he nursed from a mother goat.

One fateful day, a big roaring tiger suddenly appeared, scattering the herd of goats, leaving the baby tiger frozen in front of this huge tiger. As the large tiger let out its thunderous roar, the baby tiger emitted its timid bleating sounds. The huge tiger could not believe its ears. He roared again. The same reply from the baby tiger was again a ridiculous bleating sound. *This is awful!* the large tiger thought.

He grabbed the baby tiger by his neck, trotted him down to a nearby pond, and held him out over the water. The water was still and became an instant mirror to the baby tiger. It was amazing! The baby tiger saw for the very first time that he looked more like a baby tiger than he did a baby goat.

Nonetheless, when placed back on all fours on the ground, the only sounds he could produce were those same weak, feeble bleating sounds. Each time this happened, the mature tiger would cuff him with one of his big paws on the side of the head and let out a loud thunderous roar. Before long, the baby tiger also began to make noises that sounded more and more like a roar than a timid bleating sound.

Then the big tiger began to introduce the baby tiger to meat from prey and discouraged him from eating the grass. In short time, the baby tiger had changed and began acting like a tiger!

*   *   *

Why did this happen? It happened because God created the baby tiger to be a tiger and not a goat. When the mature tiger came along, confronted him, and showed him what he was supposed to be like, it lovingly brought out of him or transformed him to become what he was intended to be—a tiger!

This story has been stuck in my mind for over twenty-five years since I first heard it. I wanted to share it with you because what happened to the baby tiger sums up how *The Reset* can transform your life.

Many other books are available that go into much more depth explaining the transformative nature of positive self-talk. However, this book does not share the primary focus of many of those books, which is "me getting more of what I want to please me and make myself more successful." The approach taken here is for you and me to *reset* our thinking back to the way God originally created us to think and live. I also keep it simple because I want you to have something that is practical and easy to use, and that will help you see yourself as God sees you. We will utilize positive self-talk in *The Reset* from a completely God-centered and God-inspired perspective. You ultimately do become what you think about yourself, so why not let your thoughts about yourself line up with what God Himself thinks and says about you?

The seven biblically based self-talk *Reset* statements will work best for you if you memorize them and say them over and over to yourself each day. These simple, but powerful phrases will begin to replace and eventually eliminate any negative or erroneous ones that have misguided your life up to this point. I get excited knowing that in just a few short days and with a little honest effort by you to change your daily personal self-talk, you will discover that there is a tiger also waiting to emerge in your life.

Where Did This Negativity Begin Anyway?

The earliest pages of the Bible tell us that God created the first man and woman, Adam and Eve, in His image. Nevertheless, they disobeyed God and made a deliberate choice to try living life their own way. It was not a good idea then, and we all still have an inward bent to make the same mistake.

Therefore, like all the descendants of Adam and Eve, we have also suffered and reaped similar consequences of making that same choice. The common biblical concept for this do-it-my-way lifestyle is being *lost*. When we live our lives and make our daily choices based on our images of ourselves rather than on God's image of ourselves, we create an undeniable separation between God and ourselves. As a result, our rightful relationship with Him is *lost*.

What you are feeling and experiencing in your life right now may be part of that same story playing out in your current circumstances. Yet God has never given up on you. He has never stopped loving you. You are still on his mind even though it may have been quite awhile since you thought about Him. And while your life today may be far from where God would want you to be, His thoughts toward you are still good thoughts. Did you get that? *While your life today may be far from where God would want you to be, His thoughts toward you are still good thoughts!* If you will accept His offer of a *reset*, God has already initiated the transformation of your life that you need and that you are perhaps desperately longing for.

You are now probably thinking as most people do that you could never be good enough to please God. Congratulations, you are so right about that! Yet, that misguided approach is what many religions are all about, trying to be good enough to earn God's favor and approval. In most religious efforts, men and women will search and strive for many different ways to climb up to God. It never works. It never works. I'll say it again, it never works!

Our 28-day *reset* journey begins by understanding that God initiates it all. He bends down and reaches out personally to you first with His unconditional love. He knows your name. He knows the state of your life right now. However, His thoughts about you are good, no matter what you are doing in your life today or what you have done in the past.

That is why I want you to continue learning today and repeating our first life changing self-talk statement from yesterday. However, I want you to do one more thing and add two additions to your first self-talk statement. Your complete statement on your index card should then read:

> I am on God's mind again today.
>   (even if I just messed up)
>
> I really do matter to God, and He is always
> thinking precious thoughts about me.
>
> Today, I will let God be on my mind too.

Have your first *Reset* card with you as much as possible and throughout the day, look at it, read it, say it aloud, and learn it. Make sure you also have Romans 12:2 and Psalm 139:17 on the back of your card. These are the words of God, and you can definitely believe what He says.

This completes our first statement by adding the parenthetical phrase that can be helpful after the many occasions when you and I will mess up. In this life, we will always be prone to falling short or missing the mark of God's standards. When we do mess up, God's thoughts about us will remain constant, and He will love us no less. Now, this does not mean that God will make an exception and approve of our behaviors that are contrary to His holy standards for us, but we will always have a special place in His heart when and if we choose to accept His offer of forgiveness (this will be another *Reset* later in our journey). Furthermore, once we realize that we are always on God's mind, in response to Him, we will find ourselves wanting to have God on our minds too!

For review today, simply make sure that you have completed your first *Reset* card with the statements on the front and the two supportive biblical verses on the back. Again, repeat them to yourself as often as possible. If possible, say the *Reset* aloud to yourself so that you actually hear your voice speaking to you. Emphasize different words each time to appreciate the full meaning of each word. As you learn the statements and the verses better, try writing them out again on a clean sheet of paper. Probably after a few days, you will even be able to recite them over in your mind while you are doing everyday activities like driving your car, working out, or eating your lunch. Keep repeating them until you know them well and they begin to transform you and change the way you think.

Review

Reset #_____.

I am on _____ mind again _____.
  (even if I just _____ ____)

I really do _____ to God, and He is always _____ precious _____ about me.

Today, I will let _____ be on my _____ too.

"Let God transform you into a new person by changing the way you think" Romans 12:2.

"How precious are your thoughts about me, O God. They cannot be numbered" Psalm 139:17.

Let your desire for change begin to help you believe these verses, and remember that despite what some may say, God's word is true and reliable. Then begin to let these words dislodge the old negative thoughts that you may have stored for years. Be willing to let go of them and pray today's prayer often until your new thoughts begin to take root and replace the old ones.

Where you are today in life's circumstances is a fact, but it is also a fact that with God, there are no impossible situations. You have probably already tried to live life your way. Why not give God's way a chance now? Start today. Be hopeful. God's word says, "Come close to God, and God will come close to you" (James 4:8). If God said it, then it is a promise that you can count on and one that you need to take advantage of today!

Today's Prayer

Dear God,

Thank you for loving me right where I am today. I have tried before to straighten out my life, but usually it has always been on my own terms. I have acted much differently from the way I know you created me to be. Because of that, I have made mistakes and have some scars to prove it. I never really understood the principle of how I think about myself affects my life. I can keep thinking about life my way or I can learn to think about life your way. It has been easy for me to push you out of my life and out of my thoughts, but with your help, I want to give this *reset* journey a chance. Help me to change my thinking. Help me to see myself as you see me, and help me to accept your good thoughts about me. Right now, God, I want you to be on my mind too! Amen.

Day 5

We All Love Rescue Stories

He reached down from heaven and rescued me;
he drew me out of deep waters . . . he rescued me because he
delights in me. Psalm 18:16, 19

William Penn, the founder of the state of Pennsylvania, lived from 1644 to 1718. It is widely held that he stated these thought-provoking words: "Right is right, even if everyone is against it; and wrong is wrong, even if everyone is for it." Wow! Does our generation ever need to hear those words?

Here in America today, we are rapidly losing our focus on what is right and what is wrong. This has primarily happened because, in recent decades, we have again forgotten our unique heritage and have repeated the pattern of previous generations, going all the way back to biblical nations. As mentioned on Day 1, history is full of examples of nations and leaders that have turned their backs on God, ignored His truth and wisdom, and charted their own courses and destinies.

Which Way Is American Turning?

The uniqueness of America today is that there are many more factions vying for the very heart and soul of our nation than in any other period of our two-hundred-plus year history. Our generation is testing and challenging almost every aspect of traditional American culture and values. In many areas of public debate, those who openly deny God's existence and His rightful authority in our lives are dangerously undermining the traditional moral fabric that been the strength of America since its inception. The more our society takes God out of our collective thoughts and daily consciousness, the more our nation suffers the natural consequences of turning our backs on Him.

Biblical and secular history demonstrates that nations will reap either blessings or curses depending on whether they follow or disregard God's ways. Most of us are familiar with the principle of "you reap what you sow." In summary, our American way of life is now reaping the consequences of our collective poor choices of turning away from God and following our own misguided thinking. God's Word is still true, and it always will be whether or not you or I choose to believe it. Just like we cannot break the law of gravity, but we can be broken by it if we fall from a high place; we also cannot change the ways of a holy God, but our lives and our country can forever be changed by disregarding what He says.

You and I must remember that "right is right, even if everyone is against it; and wrong is wrong, even if everyone is for it." Truth does not change with the passing winds of time or for the whims of a rebellious and godless culture. That is why I am basing our seven self-talk statements for this personal *reset* journey only on what God's Word says. Furthermore, if you are going to take this journey seriously and if you are honestly looking for a positive *reset* in your life, would you not want it guided by unchanging and reliable truth? Just as nations can lose their focus on what is right, so can we as individuals. When someone takes an ill-fated turn down a wrong road and becomes lost on their journey, isn't that a great time for a rescue to occur?

To Be Rescued or Not

Let's face it, many great stories or events are inspiring to us because they involve an improbable rescue of some sorts against all terrible odds. I can think of several recent events that made the worldwide headlines. There was the captain and his crew of a merchant ship that lawless pirates held captive for ransom on the open sea. After a tense standoff, we were all relieved when US Navy sharpshooters took out the pirates by gunfire and were able to set the captive hostages free.

More recently in Chile, tons of dirt and rock tragically trapped coal miners deep in the bowels of the earth. Against all hope for many weeks, experts attempted every possible rescue effort to locate and save the men. People offered desperate prayers in many languages all around the world. Even countless number of rescue setbacks did not deter our collective hope for a rescue. Unspeakable joy finally erupted when one by one, the entrapped miners were brought up to safety in a newly designed, small cage and reunited with their families and friends! Large television screens all around the world captured the scene live and for a moment, the nations of the world acted like a big family celebrating the dramatic rescue story.

In these and other countless movies and books based on real or fictional hostage or extremely dangerous events, we find ourselves desperately cheering for the daring and successful rescue to take place. When it happens, our joy mysteriously bonds us with the rescued.

Sometimes, the rescue that we hoped for does not occur. Most of us can recall the awful, gut-wrenching, sick feeling in our stomachs that our nation experienced when we repeatedly viewed the Challenger space shuttle tragically exploding on live television and realized that there would be no possible rescue for our astronauts. Our hearts grieved deeply for the families as they stood in total shock and disbelief, staring upward at the errant trails of white smoke from the booster rockets framed forever in the blue sky above them.

That same sickening feeling repeated itself horrifically for weeks after the unthinkable day of 9/11. We watched the brave efforts of public servants and volunteers to locate and rescue possible survivors of that evil and wicked act of terrorism. We unashamedly cried tears of sadness for those hopelessly buried, but we still had occasional tears of overflowing joy and renewed hope with the miraculous rescue of a few.

There Is Even Better News of a Different Kind of Rescue

I bring up this universal hope of rescue that we all share to remind you of the faithfulness of God's character and that He is always our reliable rescuer. His Word contains the truth that we all need to hear, no matter what the growing number of misguided skeptics in our culture will say. The Bible gives an honest presentation (both the good and bad) of biblical history and of God's interaction with the various people groups and nations of the world. It shows the faithful and reliable consistency of God's desire, ability, and willingness to rescue those who have been enslaved and entrapped in their own self-willed rule. *What He wants most from you and me today is a personal relationship based on His unconditional affection for us and our acceptance by faith of His unmerited grace and forgiveness for our sins.*

I need to tell you that God's heart is broken when we choose to turn our backs on His relentless love for us. On the other hand, His greatest pleasure comes from our choice to have a personal daily relationship with Him. As you continue this 28-day journey, you will begin to let God transform you by changing the way you think about Him and by understanding what kind of thoughts He has about you.

Up until this point in your life, you may have classified yourself as leaning toward being either a nonbeliever or a believer in God. You might even see yourself as a person mostly against organized religion or as a person who is very religious. In either of these cases, you may have still missed the point.

It Is About a Relationship, Not a Religion

In an excellent book, *He Loves Me!* by Wayne Jacobsen, chapter 4 covers the subject, "A Father Like No Other." In clarifying the real message behind the Parable of the Prodigal Son (Luke 15), he says that the real central character in the story is really the father and not the wayward son. He also suggests that the story could easily be called, "The Parable of the Incredible Father." Jacobsen describes it like this:

> The first son represents those who run from God by indulging in their own selfish pursuits; the older son represents those who work hard to impress God with their commitment. Fearful of the consequences of disappointing God, they slave away for him. But they never come to the depth of relationship the Father wants with them . . . In the long run it doesn't matter whether rebellion or religion keeps you from a vibrant relationship with the Father; the result is still the same. He is

cheated out of the relationship he wants with you, and you never come to know how he feels about you.[1]

As you continue today in our 28-day *reset* journey, keep focusing your thoughts on *Reset* #1 and the supportive verses from God's Word. Perhaps it is still difficult for you to accept that you really do matter to God and that you are on His mind again today. But the fact is, His thoughts about you are precious thoughts, regardless of the current circumstances of your life, and they are too many to even be numbered. Wow! That means God considers you valuable, and that you are highly esteemed, cherished, and treasured by Him.

Some of your old, negative thinking may still challenge these new thoughts. If it helps, go back to Day 1 and read again the section about you being the gatekeeper of the thoughts that enter your mind. It is powerful to know that you can and do control the thoughts that gain entrance into your mind. Realize though that it will take consistent effort and repetition of your new self-talk *Reset* statements to help evict your old, negative, self-defeating thoughts. Moreover, remember to let God come alongside you to help you transform the way you think.

In a few days, you will begin to sense the changes coming in your life. God will begin to rescue you in ways that you cannot even imagine right now. Pause for a moment here and think of a rescue that would be nice to experience in your life. Then stop and just let God be on your mind for a few minutes. Visualize giving or handing that need or problem over to Him. Ask Him for help to deal with it. Soon you will sense that a brand-new, deeper relationship with God has begun and that He is willing to help and guide you in that area!

Review

See if you can fill in the blanks below. Keep your index card with *Reset* #1 and Romans 12:2 and Psalm 139:17 close by you today. Review it often. Focus on the key words and phrases. Continue to memorize the *Reset* statement first and then the biblical verses. Learn them word for word and be patient with yourself. If you will stay with it, you too will soon have these powerful new self-talk statements and verses taking up permanent residence in your mind and changing the way you think!

Reset #1

I _____ on _____ mind _____ today.
(even if ___ _____ _____ ___)

I really do _____ ___ _____, and He is always
_____ _____ _____ about me.

Today, I will _____ God be ____ ____ _____ _____.

"_____ God _____ you into a ____ _____
by _____ ___ _____ you _____" Romans 12:___.

"How_____ are your _____ _____ ____, O ___.
They cannot ____ _____" Psalm _____:17.

Today's Prayer

Dear "Incredible" Father,

Even though the world seems to be determined to turn away from you, I choose today to take a new direction and to now come back to you. Sometimes in the past, I have been rebellious, and sometimes I have tried to be religious. Either way, without you, I have often messed up and missed the mark. But you are more interested in my heart today than in my performance. I could never be good enough, even if that was what you wanted. What you do want from me right now is just me! That is why I am on your mind again today. I am valuable to you, and my life really does matter to you. You overwhelm me by your willingness to rescue me even though I could never deserve it. That's just the way you are! Help me today to be a better gatekeeper of my thoughts. When I have a negative thought, let me turn it away and replace it with a thought based on your Word. I will let you help me change my thinking one day at a time. Oh, by the way, God, today you will be on my mind too! Amen.

RESET #2

Day 6

An Incredible Offer for You!

Today I am so excited about what I am going to share with you about an incredible offer from God. If you are having any doubts about whether God might be interested in helping you transform your life by changing the way you think, please don't even think about stopping your *reset* journey today. I hope that you have taken time each day to focus on and begin memorizing our *Reset* #1 and the two supportive biblical verses. Your first personal index card should be kept close by so that you can review it repeatedly throughout each day of this journey. As we add each new *Reset* statement, you will add it to your daily review. Each new *Reset* will build on the previous ones.

It is imperative that you not only read the new chapter for each day, but that you also keep reviewing and saying to yourself what will ultimately be on your seven index cards as we proceed on our 28-day journey. Do not just quickly read each chapter and close the book. Take time to also fill in the blanks in the review sections and earnestly seek God by praying the prayer in your heart at the conclusion of each chapter. Better yet, continue your own prayer to God in your own words, and use the printed prayer only as a guide. In a few days, we will actually be sharing about how God comes to you when you pray to Him.

It will also help tremendously if you can review your index card throughout the day, but especially early each morning and just before you go to bed at night. In addition, remember to say the *Reset* statements and verses aloud to yourself word-for-word as often as possible. Dwell on them and let them begin to change the way you think.

A Reminder about Your Thoughts

Remember too that on some days your old thoughts or feelings may try to make a comeback and want to move back into your head and heart. They can be quite stubborn to leave at first. Nevertheless, once your new self-talk thoughts, based on God's Word, begin taking up residency within you, you will begin to sense some awesome changes taking place in your thinking. Even if you don't feel much different now on Day 6, trust the full process of how our thoughts work to change our actions or our behaviors. Go back and reread the section in Day 2 about how our thoughts form our core beliefs, which in turn affect our attitudes. Our attitudes then affect our feelings, which begin to play out more and more through our day-to-day actions or behaviors. It will take days and weeks of resetting or retraining the input process of your thoughts to realize the transformational results of your new attitudes, feelings, and actions. However, keep in mind that your responsibility now is to simply yield your thoughts to God and let Him transform your life by changing the way you think. As we introduce each new thought, just keep reviewing and memorizing each *Reset* statement.

We will now continue and share another powerful promise from God's Word and then tomorrow, we will introduce *Reset* #2. At the end of today's reading, you will want to use the back of a second index card to write out our new verse and add it to your daily review.

Too Good to Be True!

In our culture, hyped-up offers to buy a variety of products or services bombard us every day. Slick marketing targets us with all kinds of promises made, with the primary goal of getting us to part with some of our money. Open up today's local newspaper and you might be enticed by a buy-one-get-one-free deal. You will probably find a car dealership advertising that they won't be undersold. Some store may be offering a gift, free to the first one hundred customers at their early-bird opening. On the other hand, turn on your TV and hear about the amazing and incredible glue that will hold anything together.

There are also products promoting healthier hair and skin, and, of course, the products that will shape up your body and your figure. Let's face it, there are so many promises marketed to us that we are naturally skeptical about most of them. I hate to admit it, but I have responded and been gullible with a few such disappointing offers and you probably have too!

That is why many of us in today's post-modern world have grown somewhat skeptical about even God's promises or offers. Religion or church has often deeply disappointed us when we were seriously looking for answers to our life's circumstances. Furthermore, our own close family or friends have let us down so often that we now don't highly value their particular brand of faith either. All we can say about that is, "What is new?" Most of us have already concluded that people will always disappoint us to some degree.

However, this 28-day *reset* journey is not based on what other people say or do, but it is based solely on what God's says. If there ever were a 24/7 source of rock-solid, reliable truth, to me it would be what God says!

But for many people today, there is no such thing as God or an absolute truth. They have chosen to follow and believe another view of this world and of eternity. That is their choice, and unless they are looking for a real transformation in their thinking, they will probably not be reading this book. But as for me, and hopefully you, God's Word is something that we can trust enough to reopen and take a serious look at what it says. If that is the case for you, I have an incredible offer from God that you will not want to pass up.

The Word *Anyone*

Right now, I want you to grab a plain sheet of paper and a pen. In the next three minutes, I want you to write down and list at least twenty things that would describe yourself. Some obvious things might include your gender, race, age, physical appearance, health, and so forth. Going a little deeper, you might write down a word or two about your education, job, or occupation. You might list your political affiliation and your religious background or preference, if any. Your list could also include some good and not so good things about your personal history. Maybe you are happily married, you are divorced, or you are a single parent. You might have some kind of devastating addiction that is not good for you and is ruining your life. Maybe you have a criminal record or past that is shadowing your life every day. Perhaps you have lost your job and you are financially hurting right now. Is everything fitting together pretty well for you now, or is everything upside down in your life? Are you generally upbeat about the direction of your life, or are you disillusioned about it all? Take three minutes right now to list everything that comes to your mind. Go ahead and do it now.

*   *   *

Well, how did you do? Were you honest? Whatever your list has on it, it is uniquely your list. No one else has the same list as you. Your personal list describes only your life, the good, the bad, the pretty, and the ugly. Only you and God know what is on it. So now, if you would like, you can take another moment and shred your list.

Why did I ask you to do that? It was for a very good reason. Some people, perhaps even you, find it hard to believe that every one of God's promises includes them. If they would read something in the Bible referring to a promise of God, they immediately say to themselves, "That may sound great and some people may be good enough to get it, but I would never deserve to receive something like that, not with the way I have been living!"

For some reason, it is easy for us to want to search for the small print that would exclude us from God's promises. Most of the great deals in our world of slick advertising always have the extra small print stipulations or disclaimers at the bottom of the advertisement. For example, your favorite restaurant sends you a coupon for a "buy one entrée, get the second entrée free." However, the small print at the bottom says that you also have to purchase an appetizer and two drinks, and that the coupon is only good on Mondays thru Thursdays during lunch hours, 11:00 a.m.-3:00 p.m.

Now, let's think about something else that would be absurd. Suppose that God's Word had a specific promise to bless every person in the world, but only if they met all five of the following conditions. They must (1) be over six feet tall, (2) weigh 150 pounds or less, (3) be able to run a mile in five minutes or less, (4) be able to speak three languages fluently, and (5) have never eaten at an all-you-can-eat buffet. Well, I don't know about you, but I miss the mark on all five!

Our *Reset #2* is supported by a verse in Hebrews 11, which has been called the "Faith Chapter" of the Bible. Faith is obviously a huge topic, but today our focus will shift and be on one simple word. That word is—are you ready?—*anyone.*

I like that word, because *anyone* simply means anyone! No one is excluded from anyone. On the other hand, our previous list of five qualifying things would have excluded almost everyone! Going back to your personal list describing yourself, you are probably like most people and think that there were just a few items on your list that would disqualify and exclude you from most of God's promises in the Bible. In fact, if performance were the key, none of us would qualify for any of God's promises. In this next offer from God's Word, He actually puts the small print of His offer right up front in the very first word and phrase. Are you ready for this? It is our supportive verse for *Reset #2.*

> *"Anyone* who wants to come to him must believe that God exists and that he rewards those who sincerely seek him" (Hebrews 11:6, emphasis added).

There it is, simply stated in God's Word. This truth and this promise is for *anyone!* However, it does start with one condition regardless of your list. *You must want to come to God.* He will not force Himself upon you. He never has and He never will. You may not yet know how to come to God, but you must want to. That is all. Are you still with me?

What Are You Looking For In Your Life?

I assume that you started this 28-day book journey because you had a need or desire for a fresh start in your life. Maybe you are desperate and you are looking for some new hope in what you currently think is a hopeless situation. Perhaps you sense that something big is missing in your life and in your relationships. Going back to our earlier illustration about the baby tiger, you find yourself bleating through life like a little baby goat when you were created to be a roaring tiger. You sense that there is a much greater potential in your life than what you are currently living, and you long to relive more of the "one shining moments" at the end of each day!

Therefore, your focus for today is to realize that God has an incredible offer that does not leave you out for any reason whatsoever. *Anyone* includes you and overrides everything that was on your list. Nothing disqualifies you except you not wanting to accept the offer. You must only want to come to Him. So right now, you must pause and settle this issue. Ask yourself, "Do I really want to come to God?" If you do, then listen again to James 4:8. We could call it the small print or conditions to all of God's promises. "Come close to God, and God will come close to you." This is your starting point. It is like God saying, "So, you need a friend? Come to me and I'll be your friend!" Going further, it could be like Him saying, "So, you need someone to listen to you? Come to me and I'll listen. I've got time!"

> "Anyone who wants to come to him must believe that God exists and that he rewards those who sincerely seek him."

So there it is again. Hebrews 11:6 is God's incredible offer and promise to you. *Reset #2* will come tomorrow. For now, you need to get out your second index card and write this new supportive verse on the back (leave the front side for *Reset #2*). As you continue reviewing and memorizing *Reset #1*, also begin to read aloud Hebrews 11:6 today and focus on the key words, especially the key word *anyone*.

Review

Today, I will let _____ ___ ___ ___ _____ ____.

"Let God _____ you into a new _____ by _____ the way ____ _____ " Romans ___:___.

"How precious are _____ _____ _____ ___, O God. They cannot be _____ " Psalm 139:17.

"_____ who _____ to come to him must believe that God exists and that he rewards those who sincerely seek him" Hebrews 11:6.

Today's Prayer

Dear God,

It has not always been easy, but each day your good and precious thoughts about me are beginning to replace my old and sometimes negative thoughts. I am also learning to think about you more often. I like what I am experiencing so far, but most of all, I am starting to sense your presence more in my life. This *reset* idea is now beginning to make sense. I look forward to becoming more of what you created me to be. Help me continue to be the gatekeeper of my own thoughts. When I do mess up, please forgive me. I know you will! I also know that I will always be on your mind with precious thoughts, even when I do mess up. Thank you that nothing excludes me from your promises. I am part of the group called, *anyone*. Today, I do want to come to you with all my heart! Amen.

Day 7

It's Time to Take a Stand

Yesterday we introduced the prerequisite that we must first want to come to God and that this privilege is available to anyone, no matter what is on his or her past and current life resume. I hope that you were able to capture in a personal way the full sweep of God's invitation for you to come to Him just as you are. Other family members and friends in your life may not be capable of unconditionally accepting you like this, but God is more than able. He actually pursues all of us and comes after us, whether or not we are aware of His activity in our lives. Eventually though, it all comes down to us making a choice to come and respond to Him in faith or to turn away and reject His loving gestures toward us.

You Must Decide What You Will Believe

This is where "the rubber meets the road." You and I operate with a belief system in place. Imbedded in our hearts is a core belief system that determines our daily attitudes, our feelings, our behaviors, and ultimately the resulting course of our lives. There are many crucial decisions that we must make throughout our lifetimes, but the most important thing that each of us must personally decide is what we ultimately believe about God.

Our verse from yesterday is Hebrews 11:6, found in the Bible in a book written primarily to the Jewish people of its day. However, its application is the same for all generations and all people. Hebrews 11 is the "Faith Chapter" of the Bible, and there we find a beautiful description of what faith is and a listing of some rather notable examples of men and women of great faith. The Jewish audience of this biblical book was much like the modern audience of many best-selling books today. In fact, like us, the Hebrew people were in danger of having their actions or behaviors shaped by the pressures and popular thoughts of their world rather than by the promises of God. The writer of this biblical letter was encouraging the Hebrew people to stick with the faith-inspired walk with God that they had gained access to through His holy son, Jesus Christ.

The scope of our journey will not attempt to promote any brand or denomination of Christian religion, but we will emphasize the importance of a daily relationship with God that comes from Him to us as a gift. While many in our world today will discount any notion of a God that one can know personally, that is exactly where this *reset* journey will lead you. Many other well-written self-help books offer much practical and helpful advice. However, they often limit their approaches by suggesting a false humanistic theory that we can become our own gods, and that through our own self-determination and efforts, we can have or achieve anything in life that we desire. According to many of these writers and speakers, there are no absolute truths in life, no clear moral code of right and wrong to guide our interactions with each another, and certainly no need for a personal God to be sovereign over our lives. Furthermore, many of the self-help books today would totally disregard the prominent role of faith to living one's life. To summarize, their approach is that you and I are the sole responsible party for charting our lives, setting our goals, and, through self-effort, achieving our dreams.

What Have You Decided about God?

At this point, it makes all the difference in the world what you have decided about God. While huge numbers of people in our world today have dismissed and rejected the notion of a real and biblical God, our journey embraces that same God and celebrates his involvement and sovereignty over our lives. Rather than trying to replace God and put ourselves on the throne of our lives, we will choose to leave our Creator as the rightful Lord of our lives. If we truly want to *reset* our lives, we must acknowledge His original plan for us and reclaim the life that we should be living with Him.

Again, all of us have had periods in our lives when we tried our own game plan. We deviated a little or maybe a lot from God's way and we reaped the results or consequences of our actions. Then, when we totally or partially "dethroned" God, we began to alter our internal self-talk, which gradually changed our core beliefs. You know what happened next! Our altered input then changed our core beliefs. Our core beliefs affected our attitudes. Then our attitudes affected our feelings, which played out in our daily behaviors or actions, which in turn produced the net results or consequences in our lives.

Let us nail something down right here. The point of view that I am about to share does not come from me, and I do not want to sound too harsh in quoting it, but let me simply state what the Bible says about people who choose not to believe in God. Are you ready? "Only fools say in their hearts, 'There is no God'" (Psalm 14:1 and 53:1). I guess on this subject of believing in God, you are on one side of the fence or the other! Which side of the fence have you been on for most of your life? Today is a good day to make sure you are on the right side of the fence. Read that verse again. It is a clear declaration of how important it is to believe in God, and this *reset* journey concurs with that premise.

Now think about what you have believed about God up to this point in your life. What you have believed about God has been a subtle part of your self-talk to yourself all through your life. Furthermore, your concept of God is most likely similar to what others close to you have thought about Him. That concept may or may not be what the real God of the Bible is like. This *reset* journey will hopefully help you on a personal level discover and get to know God as He is revealed in the Bible. The good news for you today is that He wants to have that personal relationship with you too.

It Starts with What You Believe!

At the end of today's reading, you will write out *Reset #2* on the front of your index card from yesterday. What you believe makes all the difference in the world, especially in this process of letting God transform you into a new person by changing the way you think. The word *believe* is a difficult word to define. Sometimes we use the word in context of something we can visually observe. I could say, "I believe it is going to rain soon because of the way those dark clouds are rolling in." On the other hand, I might use the word in the context of something that I have prepared for. "I believe I have studied the material enough to pass my exam tomorrow."

The word *believe* can also be used in situations where there is no visible object to observe. It then takes on the idea of trust—to put faith in something that we cannot see, to place confidence in a person or thing, to be absolutely certain or convinced of something occurring before it actually happens, or to accept something as true beyond all doubt.

Now, let's look back at our verse from Hebrews 11:6: "Anyone who wants to come to him must believe that God exists and that he rewards those who sincerely seek him." If you were to do a study of this verse, you would discover that many commentators share an opinion that what we have here is an absolute truth with universal application. Coming in the context of the "Faith Chapter" with so many notable examples of real men and women who discovered this life of faith, this verse deserves being lifted up and highlighted for all to see. One commentator, F.F. Bruce, sums up the verse well. "Those who approach Him (God) can do so in full confidence that He exists, that His Word is true, and that He will never put off or disappoint the soul that sincerely seeks Him."[1] To carry the thought a little further, we can also say that the reward of those (anyone) who come to Him and seek Him out is the joy of simply finding Him!

Here is another crucial point to embrace. *Believing is the prerequisite to receiving.* The relationship that God offers you during this *reset* journey comes only by faith. That is the kind of faith or belief mentioned above that does not necessarily have an object to observe, but we can place our absolute confidence in God, whom we cannot see. To close this thought, hear the descriptive opening words of the "Faith Chapter." "Faith is the confidence that what we hope for will actually happen; it gives us assurance about things we cannot see" (Hebrews 11:1).

Reset #2

Now, on the front of your second index card, write out the following *Reset* self-talk statement. (Hebrews 11:6 should already be on the back of this card.)

I believe that God exists, that His Word is true, and that real joy and strength are my rewards for seeking Him.

As before, write out *Reset #2* word-for-word. Read it aloud to yourself repeatedly. Focus on each word and contemplate key words and phrases. Continue reviewing *Reset #1* and its verses. Now your goal is to begin adding *Reset #2* and its verse to your memory. Keep both index cards handy for review throughout each day. Perhaps make an extra set to have at work or in your car. I hope you are starting to see some progress in the transformation of your thoughts. God is faithful to do what He says He will do. "Come close to God, and God will come close to you."

Review

For review today, try to write out *Reset #1* and its two verses without looking (or looking much!). You could do this on a blank index card to serve as your suggested duplicate card. Remember that our ultimate goal is to know each *Reset* statement and its Bible verses word-for-word and consistent review is the only way to know them well. So take a little time each day and learn your *Resets*.

Now fill in these blanks to complete *Resets #2*.

I _____ that God _____, that His Word is _____, and that real joy and strength are my _____ for seeking Him.

"Anyone who _____ to come to him must _____ that God exists and that he _____ those who sincerely seek him" Hebrews ___:___.

Today's Prayer

Dear heavenly Father,

I realize that for me not to believe in you would be foolish. While many people have chosen to live in denial of you and your Word, I choose to believe that you exist and that the Bible is trustworthy and true. This is where I will take my stand, even though some may laugh and ridicule me. When it comes down to your word or theirs, I choose to listen to your word, and I will let it begin to guide the new thoughts that I have. Thank you again for making such a gesture to reach out to me with your kindness and unconditional love. Each day, I now sense that I am on your mind and that you are really thinking about me. That makes me want to think about you more often too. Please continue to help me *reset* and change my thoughts daily, even when I occasionally still mess up. No one has ever cared for me like you. I do believe by faith that you exist and that the Bible is true. I am beginning to experience the rewards of seeking you and the joy of finding you! Amen.

Day 8

A Reliable Source You Can Count On

Your eternal word, O Lord, stands firm in heaven. Your faithfulness extends to every generation, as enduring as the earth you created. Your regulations remain true to this day, for everything serves your plans. Psalm 119:89-91

Almost every day when we watch television news, whether it is on a cable network or a local channel, we will witness a live report from a reporter who is on the scene, giving the details of a particular unfolding story or event. It might be any kind of story, perhaps an important vote is coming up in Congress, a big break has come in a long investigation of an unsolved crime, or there is the possibility of a live news conference announcing an impending scandal in the life of a major political figure. In the flow of the breaking news alert, we will often hear the reporter saying something like, "Unidentified sources have leaked this late-breaking news to us, and we are now trying to confirm the reliability of our sources. If this information holds true, we might see further shocking developments in this story." In the rush to get the story out, sometimes reporters have been known to go on air with the information from their anonymous and unidentified sources without taking due diligence to verify their accuracy.

This kind of thing also happens every day between people. One person hears a story from someone else, and soon that person is on the phone sharing the gossip with a new person, even before the information has been verified. Both of these situations demonstrate how important the reliability of shared information must be.

In our world today, we are losing sight of what truth really is. Everything has become so relative. The majority of people today ridicule the idea of a reliable source of absolute truth from God. For them, biblical truth has been replaced by a humanistic secularism, which makes truth relative to what each person, each organization, each lifestyle, and each situation that one faces in a given moment. Each person becomes his or her own authority on right and wrong. They simply dismiss as irrelevant, outdated, and archaic the notion of an all-knowing God, who has authoritatively declared that which is absolutely right and wrong for all time.

As a result, we live in one of the most confused generations of all time. We have at our disposal the most high-tech information sharing tools and devices ever. Yet life for many people today is spiraling out of control, because most of the sources of information that we receive do not include the biblical worldview of life in general, and along with that a coherent understanding and interpretation of current world events. Furthermore, even though we have so many more ways to communicate with one another at a relational level, we often communicate poorly and at superficial levels. Life is buzzing by us each day at such a rapid pace that we hardly take enough time to talk with one another meaningfully, much less eat a family meal together and enjoy real fellowship with our loved ones and friends.

It's Time to Understand Where Real Truth Can Be Found

Part of our *Reset #2* statement from yesterday states and reclaims the fact that His Word is true. This phrase may seem short and insignificant, but it is crucial for your *reset* journey. In order for you to reclaim the life you should be living, you must acknowledge and want to *reset* your thinking according to the time-honored source of reliable truth. That source is God Himself. He has revealed His truth to us through the written Word. We call it the Bible. It would take a whole book to adequately take up the subject of the Bible's reliable and its faithful authority. While there are many good books that cover this subject in detail, here we will simply declare up front our absolute trust in the reliability and authority of God's Word for living our lives. His Word is authentic, truthful, and trustworthy, and should be the primary input for the development of our overall personal core beliefs and worldviews.

Again, remember from Day 5 the quote from William Penn. "Right is right, even if everyone is against it; and wrong is wrong, even if everyone is for it." Since it is politically incorrect now to be so moralistic, I guess we have to ask ourselves, "What then is the only reliable standard for knowing what is right and what is wrong?" Obviously, in our culture of relativism, there are many different definitions of what is right and what is wrong. For many people in today's culture, a strong commitment to the authority of God's Word is considered not only narrow-minded, but also bigoted.

Our *reset* journey does not desire to engage in a debate here. We are simply declaring the foolishness of murky and ambiguous relative truth, and advocating the wisdom of returning to a personal reliance on the faithful and absolute truth of God's Word to reclaim the life that we should be living!

God's Word to Us Is Both Simple and Profound

The Bible is a compilation of many books, written by many different authors over a long period of time, yet inspired by God in its totality. The average person can read and understand its simple principles. At the same time, it can also provide an inexhaustible lifetime of study for the most scholarly-minded thinkers. However, our approach here to the truths of the Bible will only provide a basic beginning foundation to a few elementary biblical principles. Once this *reset* journey is completed, you will be encouraged to continue to grow in your knowledge and application of your newly restored daily walk with God.

God Will Speak to You Personally Through His Word

As you continue to allow God to transform you into a new person by changing the way you think, more and more of that life-changing inspiration will come from God's Word. Our *Reset #2* focuses on the biblical assertion that God exists and that His Word is true. Furthermore, His Word is personally true for you. When you begin to realize and internalize this concept, you will then begin to listen with the deepest part of your soul to the "voice" or the Spirit of God speaking to you, just as a friend would take the time to sit down and talk with another close friend.

Do you remember on Day 3 when I shared about the encouragement card that started me on my personal *reset* journey and the idea for this book? In that card, the two thoughts, "Thinking of you" and "Just thought I would say hello, for you were on my mind," caught my attention. It was not long before God's inner voice to me connected those thoughts to the passage I was reading in Psalm 139:17. It was as if God was saying through His Word to me, "David, I am thinking about you again today, and my thoughts about you are always precious and too numerous for you to even attempt to count!" After that, I began to sense that many more people like you would want to know that God also thinks about them daily and has the same good thoughts about them too.

Somewhere along the way though, most people have been deceived in their thinking about the real nature of God and His plan for their lives. I thought, *If only I could change that by somehow sharing a simple and practical way to help people allow God to transform their lives by changing the way they think.* God enabled me over many months to develop seven basic self-talk statements, backed up with supportive Bible verses into this 28-day *reset* journey.

Without the inner voice of God, something like this would have never crossed my mind. So be encouraged in your new developing relationship with God. The Bible is a vibrant, powerful, living Word, written a long time ago, but God still makes it relevant and applicable at a personal level for you today. It can become so precious to you that it becomes like God's personal letter to you. Then when you read it, believe it, accept it, internalize it, and allow it to shape your core beliefs, it becomes a modern-day tablet, not written on tablets of stone like the Ten Commandments were, but written on your heart.

In your review time each day, be open to listening for the quiet inner voice or Spirit of God to help you apply His Word to what you are currently facing in your life. Then as you internalize and commit to memory each *Reset* statement and each supportive verse, let the truths penetrate deeper and deeper each day into your heart and mind. As that happens, your core beliefs will begin to line up more and more with God's heart. Then, of course, your attitudes and feelings will begin to change. As that happens, the *reset* process will start to transform your actions or behaviors. Soon you will be enjoying the results of reclaiming and living each day the kind of life that God had in mind for you originally!

Review

Reset #____

I am on_____ _____ _____ today. (even if I just messed up)

I really do _____ to _____ and He is always thinking _____ _____ about me.

Today, I will let _____ be on ___ _____ too.

Reset #____

I believe that God _____, that His Word is _____, and that real joy and strength are my rewards for _____ Him.

See how well you have memorized our first three verses. Try to finish these.
Romans 12:2: "Let God transform . . ."
Psalm 139:17: "How precious are your . . ."
Hebrews 11:6: "Anyone who wants to . . ."

Today's Prayer

Dear God,

It is so easy to hear and listen to all the various messages coming at us in our culture today and be confused about what is true and what is not. I thank you, God, for the reliability and the truthfulness of your Word. I will let its principles and wisdom guide my life from now on. I do believe that you exist and that your Word is true! When I interact with other people who view life from a different perspective, let me recognize and acknowledge their viewpoints while I respectfully stand my ground. I will learn from now on to base my core beliefs and my worldview on what you say. It will constantly be a learning experience for me, so please be patient with me. Please forgive me each time I mess up and reward my sincere efforts to seek for you. In addition, thanks again, God, for helping me *reset* my thoughts based on what you say about me and for changing me into a new person. I am beginning to notice a difference in my attitudes and feelings, and even my actions are beginning to change too!

Whenever I am prone to forget the source of all truth, help me to remember that your Word will always be reliable and faithful.

"Your eternal word, O Lord, stands firm in the heaven." Amen.

Day 9

The Rewards of God

One of my favorite old hymns of the church has become a daily tune in my heart during the writing of this 28-day *reset* journey. Thomas O. Chisholm first wrote the words to "Great Is Thy Faithfulness" as a poem in 1923, and then later that year, William M. Runyan put the words to music. This song has long been a classic Christian hymn and remains popular in many churches today despite the more popular contemporary music styles.

Take a moment with me and, as a short devotional thought for today, let's now consider a few powerful passages of Scripture that reveal the torn heart of a broken man. To set the historical context, the Babylonian armies, under Nebuchadnezzar, had invaded the Old Testament nation of Judah. Furthermore, they had laid siege to (and destroyed in 587 BC) its cherished capital city of Jerusalem. Their beloved city now lay ruined and smoldering in its own ashes. Jeremiah the prophet writes the book of Lamentations to literally lament and mourn the personal and national anguish he was experiencing in his heart for his cherished homeland.

Listen to his opening words. "Jerusalem, once so full of people, is now deserted. She who was once great among the nations now sits alone like a widow. Once the queen of all the earth, she is now a slave. She sobs through the night; tears stream down her cheeks" (Lamentations 1:1-2).

The depth and pain of the affliction is so great, to the point of breaking his heart. You and I will also face some personal tragedies and heartbreaks in this life. Those will be times of great, and sometimes exhaustive, "faith-testing." It is human nature during those trials to have some doubts and to wonder what God is doing. We may even feel like God has forgotten us.

In this book of Lamentations, Jeremiah continues to work through his emotions and feelings over his broken heart just as we must do whenever we go through hard times. Ultimately, it is his remembrance of the faithfulness of God that uplifts his hopes towards a brighter, more optimistic future. Jeremiah continues describing his despair in Lamentations 3:19-20. "The thought of my suffering and homelessness is bitter beyond words. I will never forget this awful time, as I grieve over my loss."

However, just around the corner comes the "a-ha" moment when he finally realizes that his eyes have been too narrowly focused only on the immediate pain and suffering. He has temporarily forgotten the forward-looking nature of God's never-ending and sustaining stream of grace and mercy and forgiveness. You will find my own notations in brackets.

"Yet I still dare to hope when I remember this: The faithful love of the Lord never ends! His mercies never cease. Great is his faithfulness; his mercies begin afresh each morning. I say to myself, [sounds like Jeremiah used a little self-talk here] 'The Lord is my inheritance; therefore, I will hope in him!' The Lord is good to those who depend on him, to those who search for him" (Lamentations 3:21-25).

God's Faithfulness Is Great and Never Ending!

Now back to our inspirational hymn. Thomas O. Chisholm found his inspiration and creative thought for this classic song from these passages in Lamentations, particularly 3:22-23. As you read the words below (or sing them if you know the tune), rate yourself on a scale of one to ten on how strongly you really believe in the absolute faithfulness of God. While it would be impressive (and a lie) if any of us could claim a ten, most likely, we all have much room to grow in our total reliance upon the faithfulness of God. Working against us is the ever-prevalent and over-inflated idea in our culture that we should become more and more self-sufficient and self-reliant. That is why the secular humanists in our society frown on even the mention of a nation or an individual wanting to trust and rely daily on God.

Read now the inspiring words of this classic hymn of faith and let the hope and confidence penetrate deep into your heart and mind.

Great is Thy faithfulness, O God, my Father,
There is no shadow of turning with Thee;
Thou changest not, Thy compassions they fail not
As Thou hast been Thou forever wilt be.

Summer and winter, and springtime and harvest,
Sun, moon and stars in their courses above,
Join with all nature in manifold witness
To Thy great faithfulness, mercy and love.

Pardon for sin and a peace that endureth,
Thine own dear presence to cheer and to guide;
Strength for today and bright hope for tomorrow
Blessings all mine, with ten thousand beside.

(Chorus)
Great is Thy faithfulness
Great is Thy faithfulness
Morning by morning new mercies I see;
All I have needed Thy hand hath provided—
Great is Thy faithfulness, Lord, unto me.

* * *

So What Are the Rewards of God?

Wow! What a great hymn. I believe we can find the answer to our question in the words of the hymn you just read and contemplated. To begin with, the word *reward* carries with it the connotation of a satisfying outcome, return, or result of some action or behavior that we have undertaken on our part. In *Reset #2*, we are declaring that the outcome or rewards for doing our part (which is to seek Him) is that we receive a sense of *real joy and everyday practical strength* to live a life of gladness and still be able to overcome the hardships that will inevitably come our way.

In the hymn, we can see several things related to our journeys. First, in verse one, the focus is on the steadfast nature of God's character and His compassion. Despite the present picture or temporary circumstances in our lives, God's character does not change or shift like a shadow will.

In verse two, we see the steadiness and reliability of God represented in the seasons of the year and in the precision and orderliness of the heavenly bodies in their reliable and predictable courses in the skies above.

In verse three, we find that God is also rock solid in his never-wavering promise to forgive us when we sin and to give us the gift of peace to our troubled souls. Furthermore, He promises His own guiding presence to walk with us, and that He will provide strength for each new day and give us a bright, overflowing hope for all of our tomorrows.

Finally, in the refrain or chorus of the hymn, with a great and loud melodious crescendo, the undeniable, morning-by-morning, every-single-day faithfulness of God mercies is declared. His hand provides all that we need. There is no room for doubt as we sing that last line one more time, "Great is Thy faithfulness, Lord unto me."

In God's vocabulary, we can define His grace as "receiving what we do not deserve or merit (such as salvation)." On the other hand, we can define his mercies as "not receiving what we deserve to receive (i.e., punishment for our sins)." I heard an illustration one time that compared the terms *justice* and *mercy*. It stated that justice is what you receive when you stand before the judge and he orders you to pay a fine for your speeding ticket. Mercy is what you receive when you stand before the judge and he dismisses both the violation and the fine.

If we are keen with our spiritual eyes, we will be able to see and recognize the numerous mercies that God extends to us on a morning-by-morning basis. Not a day will go by, good or bad, that God's faithfulness will not sufficiently provide for our needs. We may not immediately see with our physical eyes the evidence of His hand at work, but He will be there. I like the complete confidence of someone who once summed it up so simply. If you seek God, He will show up!

*   *   *

I hope that you are taking great comfort today in the last phrase of *Reset* #2 about the rewards of seeking God. Faith and belief are about living in the here and now, as well as the afterlife. When you stop and think about the consistent, steady, reliable, faithfulness of God, it is truly great!

You have now completed two powerful *Reset* statements to change your thinking and to have a new hope of letting God transform your life. Your thinking should now be showing some signs of going against the grain of the world's self-centered way of thinking. In other words, your thoughts and values should now be conforming more toward God's thoughts and values. At this point of your *reset* journey, my hope and prayer for you is that the time you are spending each day reviewing and thinking about what you are internalizing through memory is drawing you closer to God's heart. *You are on God's mind again today. His thoughts about you are good! Let Him be on your mind too.*

Review

I _____ that _____ _____, that his _____ __ ____, and that real____ and _____ are my _____ for _____ ___.

"_____ who wants to _____ __ ____ must _____ that God _____ and that he _____ those who _____ ____ ___" Hebrews 11:6.

Continue your review of your *Reset* #1 card. You should have it memorized fairly well by now. It is crucial that you learn each *reset* so well that they will be up for automatic daily recall in your mind later on.

Today's Prayer

O God, the faithful one!

I like the thought of addressing you, God, as "the faithful one." It is amazing to me how a simple hymn and Scripture can remind me once again of your great and remarkable faithfulness. I thank you for being so reliable and worthy of my trust. You are like a solid rock to stand upon in the storms of life. When days are a little rough sailing, help me to draw upon the fact that you exist, that your Word is true, and that real joy and strength are my rewards for seeking you. When days are good ones, help me to rejoice and to take great pleasure in the day-by-day mercies you send my way. Even on the not-so-good days, I will still delight in experiencing your faithful love and care for me each day, and at night I will continue to rest in your goodness. The joy and strength that I receive from your great faithfulness are my anticipated rewards for seeking you again today. Amen.

RESET #3

Day 10

We All Need Some Help
Getting Around in Life

Bend down, O Lord, and hear my prayer;
answer me, for I need your help. Psalm 86:1

Several years ago, I read one of the best practical books I have ever read about how much God cares for us. *God Works the Night Shift* was written by Ron Mehl, and I would highly recommend it as a must read. Since I always read books with a highlighter or pen in my hand to mark key passages, quotes, and illustrations, my copy of his book is full of personal notes and highlights. One of the best quotes in the whole book is so profound that I have written it in the margins of several personal Bibles beside Psalm 18:16, which reads, "He reached down from heaven and rescued me." You may eventually want to do the same in your Bible after you finish today's reading.

Ron Mehl was trying to simplify and give us the Bible's ultimate message in a bottom-line-type way. I think he hit the nail on the head! Listen to his summarizing conclusion.

"Doesn't the Christian life really boil down to being held by God and, in turn, holding on to him?"[1]

Sometimes a Story Tells It Best!

Today our journey takes us to *Reset #3*. You will get both the newest self-talk statement and the two supportive verses to write out on your third index card. Then we will take a few more days to reflect and absorb the full impact that this *Reset* will have on your transformation process.

A story often conveys a truth much better than a lot of talk. Again, I want to share from Ron Mehl's book. Stories about children especially get our attention, and this one is a grand slam out of the ballpark.

One day I (Ron) was visiting with this friend while he was charged with watching his granddaughter. "Watch this, Ron," he said as he swept the little girl into his arms. He stood her up against the couch. Even with her back against it, I could see it was all she could do to stay in a standing position.

Then he said, "Come to Bumpa, darlin', come to ol' Bumpa!"

The fat, spongy little legs that would barely support her while leaning against the couch absolutely wouldn't support her in the big world on her own. She took one short, tiny step, and fell into a pile of legs, diapers, and corn-silk curls. The she just grinned.

Grandpa smiled, too, but seemed a little embarrassed. He stood her up against the couch for another try.

"Come on little darlin'. Come see ol' Bumpa. Come on, sweetheart!"

Her heart was in it. Her spirit was game. Out she stepped. Down she went.

My friend laughed again, but this time was not quite able to conceal a growing fear that he might have bragged about this child's mobile abilities a tad early.

"Maybe she's just had a long day, Bumpa," I teased.

He smirked. One more try. One more pile of ten-month-old on the floor. This landing was a little harder than the others, and the toddler began to whimper. My friend reached for the standard excuse phrase.

"Aw, well, she's just tired. Too tired from all that walking she did yesterday."

Then he did what I thought was a wonderful thing. Instead of just leaving the little lady to crawl off defeated on her own, he wanted her to be encouraged by her efforts. He reached down with those big, work-hardened hands, took hold of her chubby little fingers, lifted her up, turned her around, and set her feet on top of his. When he lifted his left foot, her left foot went up. Same with the right foot. They walked around the room with a precision that would have made a Marine drill sergeant proud. An expression of assurance and delight dawned on that little girl's face. She was walking! She'd been instantly transformed from a stumbling toddler to a little woman striding the runway in a Miss America pageant. All because of Bumpa's helpful hands and feet.

She laughed with pleasure and walked with pride, too young to realize that her little feet balanced on big feet that had walked many miles, that her little hands clung to big hands that had carried many heavy loads, that her equilibrium depended on the balance of a man who'd stood in the wind, marched in mud, walked on ice, and navigated fast-moving streams in hip-waders. And all the while she was cheered along by a grandfather's heart that anticipated her needs and loved her very much."[2]

*   *   *

That story paints a great picture for us of how much our heavenly Father desires to get personally involved in our lives, to help us get up and get back on our feet, and to guide us in the way that we should be going in life. At this point in our *reset* journey, many of us may need to adjust our understanding of God and realize just how He relates to us when we reach out to Him.

If you have ever been around children, especially younger ones, you have probably noticed something common about their behavior. Whenever they need something or want our attention, whether they are lying flat on their backs in a crib or crawling around on their hands and knees, they reach up with outstretched hands to people they trust and have learned to depend on. They learn to be persistent too, and if we ignore their pleas for assistance for very long, they will take further action by tugging on our pant legs when we come within their range. Unless we are uncaring and hard-hearted, what do we then do? We usually bend over and engage with them either verbally or physically, trying to interpret the immediate need that they are expressing to gain our attention.

It Is God's Nature to Love You 24/7

In many different places, the Bible attempts to show us that we get the same kind of love and response from God, our heavenly Father, as He reacts twenty-four hours, seven days a week to our needs as His children. It is His nature to take notice of us.

Remember, we have claimed from the beginning of this *reset* journey that we are on God's mind with precious thoughts each day. I hope that this thought has already begun to transform your thinking about the deep love that God has for you.

At the same time, it is possible that some of our perceptions of God are negative ones that were formed from the real experiences, good or bad, that we had growing up with or without our biological fathers. In our culture today, the rampant number of absentee fathers and single parent homes makes it even harder for many people to have a positive, healthy image of God. Adolescents growing up in such environments are more likely to struggle and resist attempts of genuine love and nurture by significant adult figures in their lives. In my days of being a children's pastor, I witnessed this cause and effect in children's lives many times. Many adults seem to have no idea as to how their own daily behaviors affect young lives for good or bad, and often for many years, if not for an entire lifetime!

Whatever your concept of God was when you started this *reset* journey, today you must continue to allow yourself to see Him as the Bible portrays Him. If the previous input into your mind about God was negative, today you will need to toss out and evict those thoughts as false ones. Our authoritative and reliable source will again be what the Bible says about God. Remember that God is trustworthy. He is faithful. He is caring and loving. He is ever ready and present to come to you and meet you at your current point of need. Furthermore, the Bible wants you to visualize God like a loving father figure, who will take the time and notice you when you call out to Him. He will bend over today to give you the personal hands-on attention that you need.

Like the title of today's journey, *we all need some help getting around in life.* Where will that reliable help come from? God's Word gives us the answer. Look now at our supportive verses for *Reset #3.*

"Bend down, O Lord, and hear my prayer; answer me,
for I need your help" (Psalm 86:1).

"O Lord, you are so good, so ready to forgive, so full of
unfailing love for all who ask for your help" (Psalm 86:5).

While many in our culture will dismiss a personal dependency on God as outdated and an unnecessary crutch to lean on in these days of rugged individualism, you and I can be transformed and learn to live life God's way and reap the rewards of His joy and strength. As Ron Mehl said, "Doesn't the Christian life really boil down to being held by God and, in turn, holding on to him?"

In this chapter, we have emphasized the mental picture of God as bending down to us, but sometimes He will also lift us up. The older we get, we will also need to be lifted up when we have just been put down by some of the cruel realities of life.

One of my favorite pictures shows a father holding his little son up high, standing him on his broad shoulders, while firmly holding him steady around his little waist. The little boy is holding a basketball in his tiny hands over his own head and is reaching high to put the ball into a basketball hoop, which is now just within his reach. The caption on this picture says, "A father is someone you look up to, no matter how tall you grow." God will always be that someone that we can look up to and rely on, no matter how grown up and sophisticated we become.

Here is *Reset #3* for you to write out on the front of your third index card, along with Psalm 86:1 and Psalm 86:5 on the back of your card.

I now visualize God bending down to personally hear and answer me when I pray and ask for his help and guidance.

Review

Reset #1

I am on ____ ____ ____ ____.
   (even if __ ____ _____ __)

I really do matter __ ____ and He is ____ _____
_____ _____ about me.

Today, I will let ____ __ __ __ ____ ___.

"Let God transform ____ ____ a ___ person by _____
the way ____ _____" Romans ___:__.

"How precious are ____ _____ ____ me, O God.
They cannot be _____" Psalm ___:__.

Reset #2

I believe that God _____, that His _____ is true,
and that real ____ and _____ are my rewards for _____ Him.

"Anyone who wants ____ ____ ____ ____ must believe that
God _____ and that he rewards _____ who sincerely ____ ___"
Hebrews 11:___.

Write out your complete index card for *Reset #3* and begin reviewing and memorizing it along with the two Bible verses.

Today's Prayer

Dear God,

As I think about you today, I ask you to help me have a correct view of you as my heavenly Father. As a child of God, I am not ashamed to be dependent upon you every day, especially in times of great need. I acknowledge that I really need some help getting around in life! Help me learn to turn to you often, with complete confidence that you will hear and answer me when I pray and ask for your help and guidance. O God, please make yourself real to me today. I will ponder the verses for today and enjoy your readiness and willingness to forgive me and to extend your unfailing love to me. I will never deserve any of this, but I will receive and embrace it all today as your gifts to me. Help me to begin sensing your close presence in my life and to look forward to spending some quiet moments with you each day. Amen.

Day 11

God's Arms Are Never Folded When We Go to Him

Most parents can relate to this scene. The family is all excited about their long-awaited summer vacation. School is officially out for the summer. Mom and dad have had their time requested off forms approved months ago for this much-needed family vacation. The luggage is all packed and loaded, and the first few hours of those white slash marks dividing the interstate into lanes have whizzed by the family SUV. The trip will be a long one, taking almost a full day of steady driving. However, children do not fully understand the ETA (estimated time of arrival) as much as their parents do. Inevitably, one of the children will begin showing obvious signs of physical and mental restlessness from the cramped confines of their limited personal space in one of the back seats. That famous line, which is mysteriously preprogrammed before birth into all children, then comes spilling out, "Are we there yet?"

I am so excited that we have now journeyed together in this 28-day *reset* for ten days. We have made significant progress, but we still have some miles to cover. Let me encourage you to enjoy our journey one day at a time and be patient to give God the full 28 days to begin changing and transforming the way you think. It is important that you not only read each day's chapter, but that you find some moments throughout each day to reflect on and memorize each *Reset* self-talk statement word for word and the verses that support them. Make sure that you have a set of your index cards with you as much as possible for quick reviews throughout your daily schedule.

Be assured that by the end of this journey, your life and your way of thinking will be reoriented or *reset* back to the way of living that God has desired for you all along. You will then possess the ability and the renewed mindset to continue a lifelong journey and relationship with the ever-faithful God who never folds His arms when you go to Him. I hope that you have already experienced a little of the fresh start that we invited you to experience back on Day 2.

The answer that parents must honestly tell their children in the back seats of the traveling family SUV is, "No, we are not there yet; we still have a little farther to go. So let's all just be patient and enjoy the rest of the drive, because it is going to be so worth it when we finally get there."

Trust me. The rest of our 28-day ride also has some more great insights to see and to experience. We will not arrive at a final destination on Day 28, but for you, it will be the awesome continuation of your fresh start and exciting life-long journey with God.

Connecting With God Should Be Normal!

Yesterday, we introduced *Reset* #3 and the two supportive Bible verses that should now be written out on the front and back of your third index card. We have also mentioned earlier in our journey that when we personally reach the point where we are sincerely seeking God and genuinely coming close to Him, then He will respond and come close to us (James 4:8). Obviously, this *connection with God* can be an uphill challenge for some, especially if they have spent most of their lives not even talking to God. In human interactions, we know it takes time to get to know someone and to be around them for a while before we are able to start trusting them. To become close friends with them takes even more effort and time.

It is the same with having and experiencing a close daily, personal relationship with God. However, we do have a reliable record in the Bible of many men and women who began and maintained a relationship with God based on faith and trust. Not one of them initially entered their relationships with God based on their personal record of good deeds. In fact, many of the "heroes" in the Bible had some serious character issues and flaws in their career resumes. That should give *anyone* (there's that word again!) hope that approaching God is not just for "perfect" people. There are no perfect people anyway! We all have made our mistakes, and yes, sinned against God, yet He is still the incredible father who loves us and desperately wants us to come back into a close personal relationship with Him.

If you have never connected with God like that, or if it has been a while since you have connected with God in a genuine way, it is important that you internalize *Reset #3* deep into your heart and mind! God really wants to connect daily with you. You matter to Him even if your personal history and resume is something you would rather try to hide from Him. You and I both know that will not work anyway. The central message that runs throughout the Bible is simply God's ongoing effort to reach down and connect with broken and hurting people like us in this messed up world system. He did this by sending Jesus, our Savior, to mend our brokenness, bring healing to our eternal souls, and help us reclaim the life we should be living.

God Loves You So Much that He Will Even Crawl under the Table with You!

Again, I want to make a strong point here about how far God is willing to bend down to meet us where we are and to lead us on to the places where He wants our lives to go. All of us have some battle scars that we have received in life. Even as you are reading right now, you may have a few undersized Band-Aids trying to hide and soothe some recent devastating and painfully raw emotional wounds. Life can be extremely tough and cruel at times. Unfortunate circumstances can blindside us and jerk the proverbial rug out from under us. Sometimes we make our own poor choices and reap the natural consequences of our actions. Other times, even the closest people that we thought we could trust the most, will do the worst damage and inflict the most pain in our lives. In all of these situations, God takes notice because you and I really do matter to Him. Listen to another story as told by Ron Mehl about a children's teacher in his church. Anita had captured a heart like God's for a little boy in her class, and her response to his needs reminds me of how God responds to our needs as well. You will find my notes in brackets.

Anita Cadonau loves children. She recently told me about Jered, a little boy in her Sunday school class. She'd been keeping her eye on him for some time [God is always watching us too]. He was a likable child, but seemed to lack confidence. And he hardly ever smiled.

One day while Anita's class was doing a coloring assignment, Jered make a mistake, inadvertently coloring outside the lines on his paper. He became so frustrated with himself that he tore his paper in two, threw it on the floor, and crawled under the craft table. When Anita went over to the table, she could hear this little guy talking to himself.

"You are so dumb! You can't do anything." [Negative self-talk.]

Anita was touched. She thought, *If he's under the table, I'm under the table*. So she got down on her hands and knees and crawled right under there after him. Jered was so upset it didn't occur to him to be surprised about this grown lady in nice church clothes crawling on the floor under a table to be with him. His nose was running and he scrubbed away the tears with the back of his hand.

"I can't color at all," he told her. "I can't stay in the lines. I always mess up. I'm just not as good at this as the other kids." [Even more eruptions of negative self-talk.]

"Who said you always had to stay in the lines?" Anita asked him.

He looked at her, considering this. It was obviously a new thought.

"You don't need to color perfectly," Anita said. "You don't have to always stay inside the lines. In fact, I think you're doing just great." She picked up his torn paper up off the floor. "May I tape your picture back together again? I'd like to keep it." [God is like this. He picks up our broken piece of life, restores us, and then He treasures us!]

The boy's eyes widened in disbelief.

"You did a good job," she told him.

Jered looked down at his picture with new eyes—as if he were seeing a Van Gogh or Picasso for the first time.

"Well, sure," he said solemnly. "You can keep it if you want to."

So she did. After they crawled out from under the table, Jared watched as she carefully smoothed out the picture and taped it back together. That afternoon she took it home, put it in a frame, and hung it on her wall. Now, whenever she sees it, she remembers to pray for a little boy who feels so badly about himself. In class, the table incident seemed to be something of a turning point for Jered.

[God has a turning point for each of us too.] He began to show a little more confidence in himself. He even began to smile now and then.

Anita's decision to crawl under the table wasn't as spontaneous as it might have seemed. In fact, she'd been watching this boy for some time. She'd noticed little things about his facial expressions and his responses. Before Jered ever tore and crumpled up his picture, his wise teacher realized there was something torn and crumpled in his heart. And as he'd colored that day, she'd seen his face turn red. She'd seen his frustration mount. She's seen his eyes fill with tears. By the time he dove under the table, she was ready to dive, too, without hesitation.[1]

*   *   *

Wow, that is a remarkable story! Now see the bigger picture. God came down to earth in human form in His only son, Jesus, and He has gotten under the table with us. He has noticed all the little things about us. He has noticed our torn and crumpled hearts. He has noticed our scars and the tears that we have wiped away with the back of our hands. He has noticed our tendency not to do what is right, and often to do what is actually wrong. He has heard our frequent outbursts of inner negative self-talk. But like the story of Jered, He comes to us right where we are today and offers us our own new personal turning points. When we finally decide to open our eyes to grasp and to embrace His help and the new perspective that He brings into our lives, we are well on our way to reclaiming the lives that we should be living.

So Let God Get under the Table with You!

It may be a completely new approach for you to think about prayer this way and envision that God gets under the table with you. Through his son, Jesus, He got under the table and died on the cross—for you! Today, He still comes down to your level and meets you where you are. Where did we ever get the idea that we had to climb up, measure up, shape up, and get it all right before we could come to God?

When you go to Him, God will never have His arms folded!
Wow, can you pause for a moment and try to get a grasp around that
thought? His arms and hands will be wide open, and His response to
your approach will always be based upon his grace and unconditional
love for you, never upon your goodness or worthiness. *Ultimately,
your confidence and hope in approaching Him and praying to Him
comes not from who you are, but from who He is!*

Your fresh-start journey with God begins with a new heartfelt,
honest conversation with Him. Prayer has been made much more
complicated than it really is. Someone once said that the greatest sin
of today's church is her prayerlessness. I would guess that thought
could also describe of most of us! We often talk about prayer, but we
actually pray very little. Listen again to the personal nature and to
the deep level of trust in God that our Psalm writer has in our two
Bible verses. You too can learn to connect and talk to God in such a
personal way. It can start today with these words.

"Bend down, O Lord, and hear my prayer;
answer me, for I need your help" (Psalm 86:1).

"O Lord, you are so good, so ready to forgive, so full of
unfailing love for all who ask for your help" (Psalm 86:5).

Review

Test yourself to see how well you are doing on *Reset #1* and *Reset
#2*. Try saying them aloud or writing them out on a sheet of paper.
Be honest with yourself, and give your review time today some extra
effort on the statements or verses that need it.

Continue learning and memorizing *Reset #3* and the two verses
from Psalm 86.

There are three sets of words in *Reset #3*, which make it easier to
memorize. See if you can fill in the blanks.

I now visualize God bending down to personally
_____ and _____ me when I
_____ and _____ for His
_____ and _____.

Today's Prayer

O Lord,

Today my understanding about prayer has changed. You are so eager and willing to come down to my level when I pray and ask for your help and guidance. I am overwhelmed by the idea that you would be like the teacher in the story and would want to get "under the table" with me. Help me to change any negative images that I may have had about what prayer is and to see you now as the God who bends down to me, who is *so good, so ready to forgive, and so full of unfailing love.* I will now come to you each day not based on anything that I have done, but will confidently come to you just because of who you are. Please speak to my inner heart and let me know that you are coming to me too. That will be enough for me! I will remember that I am always on your mind, even if I have just messed up again. I really do matter to you. Your thoughts about me are always good. Today, I want to embrace and enjoy my privilege to come to you and pray. Amen.

Day 12

Go Ahead and Ask—It's What Your Heavenly Father Wants!

The Lord says, "I was ready to respond, but no one asked for help. I was ready to be found, but no one was looking for me." I said, "Here I am, here I am!" to a nation that did not call on my name. **Isaiah 65:1**

Today we continue to explore the depth and importance of *Reset #3*, which is all about connecting personally with God. Many people have tried at various times in their lives to connect with God but have failed to sustain a real relationship with Him. Perhaps you have also tried and have only become more and more frustrated in your attempts to pray or talk to God. Some have described their futile efforts to pray by saying, "He seemed so far away; I never could seem to get through the fog." Some have said, "My prayers just don't go anywhere; it is like they just bounce off the ceiling!" Others will say something like, "Praying will never work for me because my life just doesn't measure up to God's expectations."

Comments like those could come from any of us at times in our lives, but that is not how we should experience prayer. Prayer is a special privilege that we can enjoy every day, based on a real personal relationship with God. How we come into that sustained kind of relationship will be the focus of our next *Reset* in a few days.

For now though, we must strengthen our grasp firmly around the concepts behind *Reset #3*. The first thing we must be clear about in our thinking is that we do not earn God's approval. We do not live up to His standards. We do not stack up enough good deeds over time to win His favor. We do not go to this church or that church to be in the right crowd. We do not have a magic formula that is the secret to successful praying. Furthermore, praying is *not* getting what we want by having enough faith to get it.

Most people have missed the real deal on prayer and given up because they have misunderstood prayer. Many books on prayer and some television ministries have placed so much focus on praying only to ask and receive something from God, that they have missed the real intent of God is for us to pray and receive Him and His friendship in our lives as a first priority. Yes, His blessings to us are sometimes "things," but more often, His blessings to us are Him. If we are not careful, you and I can miss the real deal about prayer too.

"Undeserved Significance"

Prayer's foremost foundational truth is that God reaches down to us first. He gives us Himself and He covers our lives with what I call *undeserved significance*. Do you remember back on Day 3 when I shared the story about the conceiving moment in my heart for this book? The encouragement card that I picked up in a store for a friend read on the front, "Thinking of You." Then on the inside, it read, "Just thought I would say hello, for you were on my mind." That line reminded me of the undeserved significance that God has placed on my life.

Let it be clear, God always initiates the relationship with us. One of the best-known verses in the entire Bible begins like this: "For God loved the world so much that he gave his one and only Son . . ." (John 3:16). At the time in history when the Apostle John wrote those words in his account of the life of Jesus, the world had long already turned its back on God. God still loved the world and reached out with a plan to redeem and save it. However, it is amazing that our significance in His eyes is never reduced, no matter if we, the created, reject the Creator.

On a personal level, that means that *nothing you ever do will make you less significant in God's eyes.* God considers you extremely valuable. However, you are not deserving of that significance, nor will you ever be entitled to it because of something you try to do to earn His great favor. Many well-meaning people who faithfully attend churches mistakenly get their feelings of personal significance solely from their performance of religious or denominational rituals and activities. Without the proper understanding of the foundational principle of *undeserved significance*, many people ultimately suffer from church disillusionment and their religious zeal quickly fades. Only our undeserved significance can explain the fact that a perfectly holy God would bend down to personally hear and answer our prayers. For you, this *reset* journey is only realized in your life when you personally decide to embrace and receive freely by faith from God's heart the undeserved significance and value that He places on your life.

You Have a Special Place in God's Heart

Let me brag for a moment about my boys. My wife and I have twin sons, Jonathan and Jeremiah, who are now in their midtwenties as I write this book. For those first few years after we were married, it did not look like we were going to be able to have children. There were numerous reasons why our chances to ever have children were slim, and several doctors had told us that the odds were not favorable. However, God had His plans for us and He blessed us with two healthy boys at the same time. For us, twins became our "instant family," and we were delighted in them and in God's special gifts to us.

As new parents, we were overwhelmed with gratitude to God for hearing and answering our prayers for children in the way He did. Although we were willing to remain childless if that was His answer to our prayers, God met us where we were in those early years of marriage and graduate schooling. He nurtured our faith as a couple to believe and trust the ultimate outcome to Him. I have shared this personal story to groups before, and every time I do, I can still recall the two unique moments when God got "under the table of discouragement with me." My own long season of personal prayers about having children had left me exhausted and perplexed about God's will in this matter. Twice it happened, and both times God's presence was with me while I was jogging on the exact same stretch of a rural road. He revealed to me on the first occasion that my wife was indeed already pregnant, and then on a second occasion sometime later in the pregnancy, that she was bearing twins. Both times, it was before any test results had revealed such great news. I would jokingly tell people after those two jogging revelations that I had quit running down that particular stretch of road!

My love for Jonathan and Jeremiah grew more and more during their early formative years and is still growing. Today, on a scale of significance in my life from one to ten, it would be a hands-down ten plus for them! They have now grown up and left the nest, soaring like eagles in their chosen fields. I love them so much! I can honestly say for their mom and myself, that our love for them has never been reduced and never can be reduced by anything that they would ever do. That unconditional love for them started the first day they were born, and it will continue to flow as a constant, ever-flowing stream until the day we die. They never had to earn our love. That love is a secure, rock-solid fact, and they will always have a special place of undeserved significance tucked away in our hearts. (I might add though that it will not hurt their cause if they choose to bless us one day with some grandchildren!)

The other day as I was driving, my thoughts turned to my sons, who currently live in two different cities away from us. Although we do not get to see them as much as we wish, we still talk with them almost every day by cell phone, texting, or through Skype on the computer. We are fortunate as parents with the extremely close relationships that we have with our sons, and we thank God for helping us develop that along the way. As I drove, I began praying for them (with my eyes open, of course) and specifically for some of the needs in their lives relating to their jobs and graduate schooling. Suddenly, my heart just began to fill up and overflow with love and deep, heart-felt appreciation for both of them.

Then it dawned on me there in the car, God felt the same way about me in a much greater way. Right then, I knew and sensed that in that moment, I was on God's mind too. I was not doing anything in particular right then to ask for that kind of significance from God, but I knew instinctively that God was thinking precious thoughts about me, just like my mind was filling up with precious thoughts about my sons in a moment of prayer. The full emotion of that thought flooded over me, and soon I had to use the back of my hand to wipe away the stream of tears that rolled down my cheeks (and yes, I did look over at the other cars to make sure that no one was looking).

Actually, I couldn't care less if someone saw me tearing up. I was receiving a great blessing from the heart of God. That moment in my car was also a great reminder for me. If I could randomly think such caring thoughts about my sons, how much more does God's heart constantly leave the glory of His heaven to come down and desire to have intimacy with me?

Why Not Connect with God Today!

There are many mysteries to prayer, but there are no secrets. Anyone can pray. Just ask God to bend down and to hear and answer you. Wherever you are right now, visualize Him bending down to have a relationship with you. If you are in a terrible circumstance today and the bottom is falling out from under you, let Him come to you there too. There are no impossible situations with God! It is always too early for you to give up. Simply pray and ask. If you do not know how to ask, then ask Him how to ask. If you sincerely seek Him, God will come to you with His help and guidance.

When You Pray, God Will Open His Heaven for You

I like the verse that tells us how God once responded to Jesus's prayer in Luke 3:21, my notes in brackets. "As he [Jesus] was praying, the heavens opened . . ." As you continue in this 28-day *reset* journey, you will discover that some of the greatest moments in your life will come to you through prayer. It will be as if the heavens are opening up to your cares and concerns. Learn to visualize God opening the heavens and coming to you, and then allow His presence to infiltrate your busy day and sustain you with His strong and steady hands.

Review

(Can you tell which *Reset* statement each verse goes with?)

"Let ____ _____ you into a ____ _____ by changing the ____ ____ _____" Romans 12:2.

"How _____ are your _____ about ___ O ____. They cannot ___ _____" Psalm 139:17.

"_____ who wants to _____ ___ _____ must _____ that _____ _____ and that he _____ those who _____ _____ him" Hebrews 11:6.

"Bend _____, O _____, and hear my _____; answer me, for ____ ____ _____ help" Psalm 86:1.

"O Lord, you are ___ _____, so _____ to forgive, so ____ of _____ love for all who _____ for your help" Psalm 86:5.

Today's Prayer

Dear God,

Today I find myself praying to you about prayer. That sounds a little funny! But I do want to see prayer as my daily privilege to connect with you and to let you enter into my world. Help me to learn how to open up and pray. You know all of the many details of my life that most people around me do not even know. When I realize how much you do know about me and how much you care about me, the undeserved significance that you place on my life overwhelms me. Some days, I think I am doing pretty well and then there are days when my heart is broken and I definitely need you to "crawl under the table with me."

Thank you, O God, for allowing me to come to you just as I am today to pray and ask you about the things that are on my mind. I desperately need your help and guidance. As I come to you today, O God, I ask that you would meet me where I am and that you would draw me closer to you. Amen.

Day 13

God Is Good All the Time

God is good all the time,
He put a song of praise in this heart of mine.
—from "God Is Good All the Time" by Don Moen

Today, we will complete another segment of our 28-day *reset* journey together. Here is a good place to pause and stretch our legs, so to speak. It will also help us to reflect and take notice of the progress that we have made so far. *Our daily focus and purpose has been to allow God to transform us into new people by changing the way we think.*

In our first three *Resets*, we have realized how much our thinking and personal self-talk shapes our lives. The cumulative thoughts and messages that we accept, internalize, and deeply believe at the core of our beings, whether they are actually true or false, good or bad, will determine who we are becoming. Words are extremely powerful! The words that you accept from others, and more importantly, the words that you accept from yourself are shaping your life for better or worse every single day.

However, *you are the gatekeeper of your thoughts*. Not only can you choose the sources of your thoughts, you can also permit or reject thoughts to have access to your mind and heart, which represents the core of who you are. In addition to this, you must learn to recognize and evaluate the credibility of each source that presents information to you for your consideration.

We all have grown up with a mixture of positive and negative input from our families, relatives, teachers, coaches, friends, coworkers, and our own self-talk. From all of that collective input, we have formulated an inner picture of ourselves that has largely become the story of our lives that we have been living out year after year.

But Does Your Life's Story Match up with God's View of You?

It is quite a game-changer when we realize that God thinks about us quite differently than most of us think about ourselves. Our first *Reset* focused on understanding the truth that we are on God's mind and about how much we really do matter to Him. No matter how badly we think we have messed up, any one of us can have our lives transformed and *reset* to God's best for us. All of us seem to love good rescue stories, and that is what God's specialty is! I hope that you have allowed that thought to penetrate your heart and mind and that it has already begun to liberate and change your life in some way on this journey.

Our second *Reset* encouraged us to take a firm stand for a belief in the existence of God and in the authority and truthfulness of His Word. As we completely embrace those two realities, we will begin to enjoy the rewards of seeking God and letting Him *reset* our lives. This way of believing and living will in many ways go against the grain of today's culture. It is a stand that you must endure with strong legs if you truly want to honor and please God with your life from this day forward. Come close to God, and He will come to you is His promise and reward. "Great Is Thy Faithfulness" will then become your daily inner song of joy and strength.

That brings us today to the wrap up of our third *Reset*, which restores our view of God as our caring, heavenly Father who personally knows our names, and who wants to come down to our level and be involved in our daily lives. The picture that we actually have from our supportive Bible verses is a God who is willing and eager to bend down and have a close, intimate, personal, one-on-one relationship with us. Even on our worst days, He will "get under the table with us" just like the teacher did with the frustrated little boy in her class. God will pick up any broken and scattered pieces of our lives, restore and mend us as necessary, and then treasure us as no one ever has!

God Is So Good

God has such an intense desire to connect with us personally. His Word, the Bible, is one of the ways that He speaks to us. Another way is in our prayers. I hope by now that you are beginning to visualize God as bending down and personally connecting with you when you pray. Keep in mind that when you pray, you are not "getting religion," but rather you are getting God Himself.

I love the words to that upbeat song quoted at the beginning of this chapter, called "God Is Good All the Time," written by Don Moen. Hear these words again and let them penetrate deep into your mind and heart.

God is good all the time,
He put a song of praise in this heart of mine.

What a joyous truth that is! *God is good . . . all the time*! One of our verses for this *Reset*, Psalm 86:5, has three such life-changing declarations. This verse has become one of my favorite verses that I think of when I go to God for a time of prayer with Him. No matter what the day's issues are that I am taking before Him in prayer, this verse covers them all.

God is . . .

- **so good.**

- **so ready to forgive.**

- **so full of unfailing love.**

Yes, God is so good, yet we often take for granted the many ways that God has blessed us all of our lives. Now, some people do not understand the difference between God Himself being good all the time, and the good or bad circumstances that are a normal part of our daily lives. Experience and reality tell us that not everything that comes to us in life is good. In fact, for much of our lives, we will have to face head on and deal often with unwanted pain, suffering, disillusionment, rejection, misunderstandings, injustice, and other forms of trouble. For some reason, many have made the common mistake and assumed that if they became a religious person, they would not have any more trouble or that God simply would not allow any hardships to come into their lives. Jesus came and taught the exact opposite. A follower of Jesus will face some of the same kind of earthly troubles that all people do. In many instances, a believer will face additional hardships and even outright persecution from a hostile world that is increasingly at odds with a biblical worldview and lifestyle.

Then what does this *God is so good* part really mean? If everyone goes through all this mess during life on earth, then what is so good about it? The answer is in God's continuous flow of faithful grace and mercy that comes to us each day and enables us to live "through it all," as Andrae Crouch, a gospel songwriter, used to sing. The remaining *Resets* on our 28-day journey will take us further down this road of understanding the overflowing, confident hope that sustains and empowers us in this life.

The Apostle Paul gave us a well-known verse in the New Testament book of Romans that gives us a bit of an anchor to hold on to here. *Romans 8:28* boldly declares, "And we know that God causes everything to work together for the good of those who love God." In a world culture that is dominated by sin's undermining dark curse, that divine orchestration of our life by God ultimately weaves together a good and beautiful story for each of us. God takes both the good and the bad events in our lives and lovingly redeems them for good throughout our earthly journey.

So let's break the verse down a little. First, what does the phrase, *God is so good* really mean? The word *so* has the connotation of "to such a great extent or to such an evident degree." The word *good* is such a common word with many facets of rich meaning, such as "competent, complete, loyal, benevolent, and kind." So digging deeper into our Bible verse, we could amplify the meaning to say, *God is to such great extent or evident degree competent, complete, extremely loyal, overwhelmingly benevolent, and lavishly kind toward us.* Let your mind dwell on that extended definition for a moment and affirm in your heart just how wonderfully *good* God is to you personally.

Secondly, God is also *so ready to forgive.* Let us pick this second phrase apart too and start by probing the word *ready.* It can be described with words like the following: "willing, eager, inclined, on the verge of, likely at any time, or available instantaneously." When I read that list, it makes me regret the times that I have been prone to wonder if God is even available when I needed Him. I think it is safe to say that we will never have to "backorder" God. *God is to such great extent or evident degree so ready or available instantaneously when you need Him.* Now to complete the phrase, He is *so ready to forgive* you. Whatever mess you have created in your life with past failures, mistakes, and sins, God is ready and completely willing to forgive them and consider them as if you had never done them in the first place; and He desires to completely restore your personal relationship with Him.

Thirdly, God is also *so full of unfailing love.* The word *full* is another rich word meaning things like "abounding, brimming, heaping, bursting, teeming, saturated, or well supplied." Now tag that concept with the following connotations for the word *unfailing*: "inexhaustible, endless, continual, constant, dependable, reliable, never failing, faithful, true, loyal, unwavering, steady, and enduring." Wow! That is almost too much to package into a comprehensible thought. But if we plug all that in, it means that *God is to such great extent or evident degree abounding, brimming, heaping, bursting, teeming, saturated, and well supplied with inexhaustible, endless, continual, constant, dependable, reliable, never failing, faithful, true, unwavering, steady, and enduring love for you.* It is amazing to think that our God bends down freely to offer all of that to us.

Prayer: Our Part and His Part

If we combined all the above amplifications of Psalm 86:5, we would get this. (Be glad I'm not asking you to memorize this one!)

O Lord, (1) you are to such great extent or evident degree competent, complete, extremely loyal, overwhelmingly benevolent, and lavishly kind toward me. (2) You are to such great extent or evident degree so ready or available instantaneously and completely willing to forgive me or to consider my failures, mistakes, and sins as if I had never done them in the first place and to thereby completely restore me into a personal relationship with you. And (3) you are to such great extent or evident degree abounding, brimming, heaping, bursting, teeming, saturated, and well supplied with inexhaustible, endless, continual, constant, dependable, reliable, never failing, faithful, true, unwavering, steady and enduring love for me and for anyone else who ask for your help.

This clearly demonstrates the vast treasures that are contained in God's Word for us to explore. Learn to read and accept the Bible, believing that what it says is true, accurate, faithful, reliable, and dependable. Now continue to use *Reset #3* and the two verses to empower your life and to reconnect again today with your Creator, who loves you so much that He wants to bend down and personally have a life-long, daily relationship with you.

Your part in prayer is to go to Him and simply believe. Whatever you take to Him, do not believe that He *will* do a certain thing for you, but do believe that He *can* do a certain thing for you, if that is His best will for your life at the time. You must simply place full confidence and absolute trust in His judgment and knowledge of the specific situations that you bring to Him in prayer.

God's part in prayer is to do whatever He wants concerning the matters that you bring before Him. You totally yield your will and limited understanding to His good and perfect sovereign will. Confidently leaving your prayers there with Him, you expectantly and patiently wait for His answers to come to full fruition in His timing. Your greatest lesson here will be to learn that your timetable is not God's timetable. Sometimes the answers will be immediate and sometimes they will come after much fervent, persistent, and patient waiting on your part. Remember that the farmer faithfully does his part in preparing the soil and planting the seed. He then waits patiently for nature to do its part and yield the harvest at its proper time. So it is with us as we do our part to plant our seeds of prayer. God then does His part to bring about the answers to our prayers in His timing and according to what He knows is best for us.

Remember that many times, the greatest results of our prayers will not necessarily be receiving the "things" that we pray for, but often we will receive the even greater blessing of Him bending down to have a close personal relationship with us. God then enables and empowers us to experience a deep, uncontainable joy and an overflowing, confident hope as we walk this sometimes difficult and hard journey called life.

Review

For a self-checkup, see how well you have memorized our first three *Reset* statements. Write out each *Reset* below and then give the biblical reference for each one. Then keep reviewing them each day using your index cards.

Reset #1.

_____

_____

_____

_____

_____

Bible Verses:_____

_____

Reset #2

_____

_____

_____

_____

Bible Verse:_____

Reset #3

_____

_____

_____

_____

Bible Verses:_____

_____

Today's Prayer

Dear God,

This is becoming such an amazing *reset* journey for my life! In just a short time, I am beginning to see and understand things that I never quite saw before. My life is literally being transformed by changing how I think. Lord, I thank you for helping me to reconnect with you and for revealing to me how much you think precious thoughts about me. Thank you for loving me and for showing me how much you want to bend down to hear and answer me when I pray and ask for your help and guidance. Help me to spend time with you and to absorb like a sponge the new thoughts that you have for me each day. God, you are so good to me. Saturate my life again right now in this quiet moment with your unfailing love. Amen.

RESET #4

Day 14

The Ultimate Reset

You have made us for yourself, O God, and our hearts are restless until they find rest in you. —Saint Augustine

Advertising and marketing promotions quite often use superlative words to describe a product or an event in order to draw the attention of potential customers. Since my wife, Pam, and I like to go on a cruise trip every few years, I was recently browsing the websites of various cruise lines. In their attempt to lure people like me, several online promotions used the superlative adjective *ultimate* in promoting their various destination packages. I assume that their marketing tactic was to plant in my mind an urgency to act now. If I was ever thinking about taking a dream cruise vacation to one of their most popular destinations, then the exotic trips on the computer screen before me were "the best of the best" and that I should consider booking one before the special offer expired. As an example, if I was planning to go on a cruise to Alaska in my lifetime, then apparently this one was the one to choose, and absolutely the best time to go. It made me wonder for a moment what we must have missed on the Alaskan cruise that we had already taken only a year earlier. It had been a wonderful Inside Passage cruise with the Coles, some dear friends of ours. But maybe we should have waited and taken this "ultimate Alaska cruise adventure."

I guess I should know by now not to entitle this chapter "The Ultimate Reset." However, please bear with me and let me justify my case. If we take a quick look at the word *ultimate* and some of its alternate meanings, it would help justify my usage of the word here. In addition to the idea of something being definitive, the word *ultimate* can also mean "crowning, greatest, utmost, or highest possible." Using that as insight, when we consider something as being "the ultimate," we are not necessarily taking away from other similar things or events, but rather we are lifting this particular one up to its rightful crowning place of highest possible significance or outcome compared to all the others.

The Big Picture Concerning Our Seven *Resets*

With that in mind, all seven of the *Resets* for this 28-day journey are critical and important, yet this fourth *Reset* is what I call *the ultimate* one! This is not another clever writer's effort on my part to get your attention. However, *without this highest possible and crowning Reset that is presented in these next few chapters, you will never realize the all-encompassing life changing potential of this 28-day reset journey.* That is why *Reset #4* is strategically in the middle of our seven *Resets*. This ultimate *Reset* statement is central to all seven. The other six revolve around and intertwine with this one. This is the ultimate *Reset*, and so for the next few days, we will present it and promote it that way. I hope that you will also see it as the crowning or highest possible *Reset* and that you will value it as such in your own life.

This *Reset* Makes Your Fresh Start Complete

Back on Day 2 of our journey, we talked about how a fresh start in life would be so nice. Life can be hard and personally exasperating at times. We mentioned the fantasy of having a big red magical reset button hidden away in the closet of our lives, that we might be able to push and restore our lives back to their original purposes and meanings. We also realized that while many of our problems are self-inflicted, and that other people will impose some of our greatest pains on us, many of the trials in our lives are just part of everyday living in this world. We also have a tendency to make things worse by our natural responses to life and our reactions to our particular circumstances. Over time our confusion tends to grow, and without always knowing why, with deep conviction we begin to sense that we are somehow missing the full potential that we should be living.

We also mentioned that in order to regain that potential, we will sporadically attempt various "spring cleaning" approaches, or self-fixes, to the situations in our lives. When they do not work, sometimes we will try the religious approach and clean up our acts to try to live better lives than most other people do. We rationalize that if our actions are just a little more moral than those around us, then we should be entitled to at least a little slack from God when He gives His final verdict on how we have lived our lives. We are comfortable opening some of our bad closets and cleaning them out for a while. That helps some, but we often keep some of our worst closet doors in double-bolted, lock-down mode. I guess we are afraid that the confrontations and battles behind those doors will be too difficult for us to handle, and so we decide to just put up with them and not deal with those areas of our lives. However, this old strategy of "out of sight, out of mind" does not solve anything. To further our cause, many of us who are well meaning may even immerse ourselves in never ending, busy church or community work, trying even yet another way to merit some heavenly favors to come our way.

While all of these efforts may yield some temporary relief, we usually remain disillusioned and unsatisfied with the overall direction of our lives. We wish that we could just push a delete button and rid ourselves of all the negative baggage from our pasts and start all over at a more innocent place. On Day 2 of this journey, we suggested a fresh start that provides that kind of ultimate *reset*. Well today, we are at that exact place on our journey where we are now ready to unveil this life transforming biblical *Reset!*

In the quote at the beginning of today's chapter, St. Augustine sums up what most of us experience much of the time. "You have made us for yourself, O God, and our hearts are restless until they find rest in you." If we are truly honest with ourselves, we all spend the bulk of our lives trying to resolve that inner restlessness and attempting to discover and achieve a basic level of peace and contentment. Different cultures promote various avenues to pursue this worthy goal, but apart from the original plan, all of them fall desperately short. Here in America, we often chase after many common recipes for so-called happiness. A short list of these includes nice careers, lots of money, luxury homes, fancy cars, prestigious memberships, drug and alcohol usage, or even a revolving carousel of new relationships to replace discarded ones. I am sure that this next statement will turn many off in our pervasively secular and humanistic American culture, but all of the above attempts to find happiness are empty, dead-end solutions to our deepest needs. *Only God can offer us the real or ultimate answer to our inner restlessness.*

God Offers You a Complete *Reset* of Your Relationship with Him through Jesus!

As we share this ultimate *Reset* with you, keep this in mind: We want you to experience the amazing transformation of having a real life-changing relationship with God; we do not want you to start acting more religious. In fact, that ultimate *Reset* only comes through what God did for you through His son, Jesus, on the cross. That spiritual experience is rooted in Christ and is called Christianity. It is sad to admit, but many people confuse being involved in a particular church denomination with having a spiritual experience with God. They actually miss most of what God really offers them. For them, they often treat their faith like a cookie jar that they can reach into occasionally for a quick snack to satisfy their temporary spiritual hunger. However, real Christianity goes deep to the core of our beings and gives us complete resolution at the root of our human restlessness. So here it is in terms easy enough for anyone to understand.

The Good News in Simple Language

The Bible is a compilation of books divided into two main sections, the Old Testament and the New Testament. The whole Bible is the story of the activities of God and His dealing with the human race since the beginning of time and His creation. The New Testament deals primarily with the era when Jesus Christ was sent by God from heaven (as foretold by the prophets in the Old Testament) to accomplish His purpose of resetting or redeeming mankind back to his original state of being right with God.

Since the fall of mankind in the garden of Eden, we have all inherited the nature and tendency of sinfulness to rebel against God and live life on our own terms. The consequence of that inherited fall is that God no longer rules in our hearts, and our deliberate choice to sin separates us from God and interferes with our ability to have an unbroken relationship with Him.

The good news is actually what the first four books of the New Testament present to us. These four books, commonly referred to as the gospels of Jesus Christ, share the same glorious story about the life, death, and resurrection of Jesus, but through the eyes of four different writers: Matthew, Mark, Luke, and John.

The Gospel in a Nutshell

To keep it simple, here is the essence of God's ultimate *Reset* presented in the Gospels in an acrostic form:

G—God created us to be with him.

O—Our sins separate us from God.

S—Sins cannot be removed by good deeds.

P—Paying the price for sin, Jesus died and rose again.

E—Everyone who trusts in Him alone has eternal life.

L—Life with Jesus starts now and lasts forever.[1]

Going back to St. Augustine's quote, the dilemma that we all face and that causes the restlessness in our hearts is the sinful nature that separates us from a holy God. Since God's Word is true and our most reliable source of truth, there is only one definitive solution for the entire human race. Only when we accept God's gracious offer and ultimate *reset* of forgiveness through Jesus will our hearts be restored to their original, restful, and peaceful condition.

So What Is So Good about the Good News?

Here's the bold headline scoop about this good news. Andy Stanley summarizes it best in his little book called *How Good Is Good Enough?* He says, "Good people don't go to heaven. Forgiven people go to heaven."[2] The good part about the good news is that I can never *earn* God's favor. I can never do enough good deeds. I only have to *accept* God's favor and His gracious offer to *reset* my life, through what His son, Jesus, did for me on the cross back on a rugged hillside in Jerusalem" (emphasis added).

Reset #4

Write the following on your fourth index card. Begin saying this *Reset* to yourself and focus today on the words *receive* and *embrace*. Tomorrow we will continue exploring other aspects of this wonderful gift from God,

> I receive and embrace Jesus as my personal Savior, and I now enjoy my relationship of being made right with God forever.
>
> I am a friend of God based on grace and forgiveness.

Review

As we continue adding new *Reset* statements, it is important that you have memorized the previous statements. At this point on your journey, you should challenge yourself to having *Resets* #1-3 down word-for-word and be continuing to add the Bible verses to your memory. Just before you go to bed tonight, see if you can say the first three *Resets* to yourself and add the verses in if you can. Remember that constant repetition each day will soon produce results. Make sure you are memorizing the *Resets* exactly as they were given.

Now fill in the blanks from our newest *Reset*.

Reset #____ (this is referred to as the "_____ *"Reset*)

I _____ and _____ Jesus as my _____ Savior, and I now enjoy my relationship of being _____ _____with God forever.

I am a _____ of God based on _____ and _____.

Today's Prayer

O God,

I find myself today almost overwhelmed at the magnitude of your love and desire for me to be saved from my sinfulness. While I was trying to live life my own way and not letting you rule in my life, I was restless and miserable inside. Now you come and offer me a fresh start, to forgive me for all my sins, and to become my friend.

Although I want to be a good person, I realize that I can never be good enough to earn your favor. So by faith, I want to accept your gift of complete forgiveness, based on what Jesus did for me on the cross. He has paid the full the penalty for my sins. I acknowledge my sins, and I now ask for your help to repent and turn away from them. Please forgive me and give me a fresh start and a clean heart. I receive and embrace Jesus today as my personal Savior, and I now enjoy my relationship of being made right with you forever. Thank you for this amazing gift! Amen.

Day 15

The Four Most Important Words
You Will Ever Say!

Then I called on the name of the Lord: "Please, Lord, save me!" **Psalm 116:4**
Everyone who calls on the name of the Lord will be saved. **Romans 10:13**

On October 13, 2004, I had to call upon the Lord in a life-or-death emergency in a split second. I was traveling alone in a midsize car north on Interstate 85, just a few miles from the city limits of Durham, North Carolina. It was in the middle of the afternoon, and the traffic was moderate as the darkened storm clouds ahead of me suddenly started to unload their blinding sheets of heavy rain all at once. My windshield wipers began their frantic, maximum-speed efforts to assist my diminishing vision of the road ahead. On the horizon in front of me, I could just barely make out a slight break in the thick cloud formations. Thank goodness, it would only be a storm of short duration! In just another mile or so, driving conditions would be back to normal again.

As I adjusted my speed downward to something safer for the current road conditions, I simultaneously noticed a beautiful full rainbow beginning to extend its colors from left to right directly in front of me. While all this was happening outside, my CD player was continuing to play the upbeat worship music that I had turned on a few miles back. The music must have subconsciously put me into a worship mode, because as soon as I saw the rainbow, I remember saying aloud, "That's a beautiful rainbow, God!"

Then everything suddenly changed all at once. A white, medium-size box truck was passing me in the left lane, spraying a massive wall of blinding mist from his unshielded huge rear truck tires. Immediately, I could barely even see a few feet ahead of my car. At the same time that I was now straining to see anything at all through my windshield, the white truck drifted into my lane. I instinctively tapped my brake pedal lightly to avoid a collision with the rear end of the wayward truck. However, instead of slowing down as expected, my car suddenly lifted itself up off the asphalt, hydroplaned sharply to the right, and plunged quickly down a steep embankment at full speed like a derailed, runaway train car. The first thing that I remember seeing flash by me on my driver's side of the car was the wrong side of a highway information sign perched atop a steel pole. I knew immediately that I was in a dangerous and helpless situation. My hands still gripped the now useless steering wheel, almost as if they had been superglued there.

To this day, I vividly remember exactly what I did next. With a steady calm that only could have come from the Lord, who I instantly sensed was in the car with me, I said aloud, "Please, Lord, protect me!"

The rest of my thrill ride was quite interesting. I recall feeling the car change directions several times as it continued to fishtail and plunge both forward and downward away from the highway above me. The distinctive sounds of smaller tree branches and underbrush kept clawing, scraping, and ripping parts and red paint off the exterior of the car. In those few flash moments, I felt as helpless as I have ever felt in my life. All I could do was wonder what object would finally bring my raging, out-of-control car to a stop, and would I even live to know what it was?

The answer came quickly. A cement drainage ditch for storm water runoff finally stopped me "dead in my tracks." I know that phrase sounds ironic to use here, but my car's front bumper miraculously plunged downward and came to an immediate stop in that shallow cement ditch. My seatbelt immediately tightened its grip around my waist and on my upper chest, hugging me securely in my seat. When I finally lifted my head and peered up through the mud-splattered and debris-covered windshield, I was amazed to see that I was only a foot or two away from what could have been a direct, head-on hit with a solid, two-foot-diameter pine tree.

When I returned to the scene a few days later to take some pictures, I saw the tire tracks in the mud where my car had actually crossed back and forth across that cement drainage ditch at least four times before coming to a stop. A heavily wooded area of pine trees was only a couple of feet to the immediate right side of the ditch. I discovered and retrieved several pieces of side paneling and other undercarriage parts lying right beside the base of some of those stalwart pine trees. Without a doubt in my mind, it had to have been the hand of God that kept pushing my car away from a sure, life-threatening impact with one of those big pine trees!

When I had eventually climbed out of the car unscratched and made my way up the wet and muddy embankment to flag down some assistance, I could recall my ever-so-brief emergency prayer just a few moments before. I thanked God right then for His protective presence. Now, the hardest part of my unplanned roadside excursion was calling my wife on her cell phone and telling her that I had just wrecked her car. Oops!

God Has an Even Better Rescue Story for Each of Us

The reason I tell that story is that it is so similar to the four most important words you and I will ever say in our lives. We discover them in one of our verses for this ultimate *Reset*. Psalm 116:4 says, "Then I called on the name of the Lord: 'Please, Lord, save me!'" That is a short prayer, but it is the most powerful and life-changing prayer you will ever pray. In yesterday's chapter, we shared the basics of God's offer to us in an acrostic using the letters of the word *gospel*. It might help to go back and review that easy outline again. Whenever you come to the place in your life where by faith you accept those basics and really desire the life in Christ that God offers you, then a simple, sincere prayer asking Him to save you will suffice. However, it is also important to verbalize to God not only our sincere sorrow for our sins, but also our intentions to turn away from the sinful tendencies in our lives. The theological word for that is *repentance*.

God's spiritual rescue story is usually a little different for each person. However, each one of our stories must somehow include these four most important words, "Please, Lord, save me!" When you and I honestly repent and call out to God like that, then His gracious gift of complete forgiveness is ours.

My Spiritual Rescue Story at Age Nine

I was only nine years old when I asked God to save me during an annual children's summer church program. As I look back now, I remember the initial feeling of cleanness that I felt in my heart. Of course, as I continued to grow up, there were many spiritual lessons to learn and more sins to confess and for which I would have to ask for God's forgiveness. However, at age nine, God sealed my eternal destiny with Him forever through the Lord Jesus Christ on the cross. I accepted God's plan that summer to receive and embrace Jesus as my personal Savior and to enjoy my new relationship of being made right with God forever. My spiritual *reset* restored my relationship with God when I was nine years old, but I now continue receiving and embracing Jesus, my Savior, each day of my life. That keeps my relationship with Him fresh and invites Him into my daily journey.

Looking back before I was saved, my childhood had been a routine one growing up in North Carolina, so there were not any major terrible sins that I knew of to confess. I did remember the summer before though when my dad discovered that one of my older brothers and some of his friends and I had pocketed some candy and bubble gum at a nearby store without paying for them. He went back with us to the store and had us apologize to the owner of the store and pay for the stolen items out of our allowance. That embarrassment cured me of shoplifting and I never forgot that lesson, but I still figured that I needed to ask God for His forgiveness. It was stealing, you know! I am sure there were other typical nine-year-old boyish sins that I needed to confess, such as telling lies, having bad thoughts, shooting a spit wad or two in school, and being disrespectful to my mom and dad. Overall, I thought I was a good kid, but I still knew in my heart that any degree of sin separated me from God. Oh yeah, even a young boy can understand the truth that "good people don't go to heaven; forgiven people go to heaven." How simple is that?

My rescue story happened a long time ago, but I am still growing every day in God's grace, learning new lessons in faith, and appreciating God's faithfulness and unfailing love more and more in every circumstance of my life.

How About Your Own Rescue Story?

Do you have your own spiritual rescue story to tell? That is so awesome if you do, and you need to share that story to encourage others along the way. Think about your story for a moment. Can you describe how your sincere prayer came out? It might not have been these exact words, but your heart cried out something like, "Please, Lord, save me!" What did it feel like when you first gave your life back to God, and do you still have the indescribable joy of being spiritually clean from your sins, or has your walk with God grown a little stale somewhere along the way? Maybe a fresh start in life and restoring a right relationship with God is what you need on this *reset* journey.

On the other hand, maybe you have not yet experienced your spiritual rescue story. I want you to know that no matter how old or young you are, no matter what your history has been, and no matter where you are in life right now, today can be the day that you choose to accept God's offer. Remember this basic truth: "Anyone who wants to come to him must believe that God exists and that he rewards those who sincerely seek him" (Hebrews 11:6). I hope that you will want to receive and embrace Jesus as your personal Savior as we continue our journey with this ultimate *Reset*. Today could be the day that changes your life forever. Consider reclaiming your rightful relationship with the one who created you in the first place and has such precious thoughts about you. Turning your heart and life over to God can start with just four sincerely spoken words. *Please, Lord, save me!*

Today Is the First "Best" Day of the Rest of Your Life!

Once you choose to receive and embrace Jesus as your personal Savior, you are immediately made right with God, and restoration and healing begins for other issues in your life. Some things will change more quickly and dramatically. Other things will require more time and process. The presence of Christ in your life makes all of the resources of God's mighty power available to you (see 2 Peter 1:3-4). All things then become possible with God in your life. You may have to work at rebuilding and restoring your character. Maybe your home and family life will need some time for forgiveness and mending to occur. You may need personal healing for some deep hurts and emotional pains in your life. Perhaps you need to seek a permanent release from a gripping addiction in your life. You might even benefit from some further professional counseling, but you can definitely start here to deal with and overcome many life situations by learning and implementing the seven *Resets* of this 28-day journey into your life. However, this fourth *Reset* is the ultimate one. Do not lightly dismiss it or discount it as only being for other people. It is for you, and your name is all over it. Look at it again and personalize it by substituting *your name* in it!

I receive and embrace Jesus as my personal Savior, and I now enjoy my relationship of being made right with God forever.

I am a friend of God based on grace and forgiveness.

Focus your thoughts today on those two words, *receive* and *embrace*. Say them aloud to yourself and use some picture in your mind to visualize what they mean. I can remember when my two boys were young and I bought them their first little baseball gloves, ball, and bat set. The gloves and the balls had the little patches of Velcro that helped aspiring little baseball players catch (receive and embrace) the plastic baseballs that were gingerly tossed underhandedly to them. I was such a proud coach when my sons made their first catches! It made me wish that I could have secretly had some Velcro in my adult softball glove when I used to roam left field and attempt to run down long fly balls!

Sometimes people make receiving Jesus much harder than it is. Actually, our spiritual enemy, Satan, is behind the scenes doing as much sabotage work as he can. However, each of us is personally responsible for our own decisions in this eternal matter, and if you will let God into your life, his power can help you overcome Satan's influence. If it helps, whether you are already a believer or if you are giving it some serious thought, maybe my picture of the Velcro gloves and balls will help you today. You might visualize receiving and embracing Jesus today in your life for the first time. On the other hand, you might visualize it in a way that helps revive the spiritual spark that you once had in your heart for God.

Embracing Jesus means that He is warmly welcomed into your heart and that your spiritual hug with Him is tight, as if you want to cherish the moment and not let go. Are you ready to do that today? If you are, then go ahead, receive Him and embrace Him right now.

Moreover, get used to it, because this ultimate *Reset* will remind you that you can now do it every day!

*   *   *

Now is the time to add two of the three verses to the back of your fourth *Reset* card. Write these two verses out using the top half of the card. Leave some space at the bottom for another verse later. They are short, they are simple, but they are infinitely life changing!

> "Then I called on the name of the Lord:
> 'Please, Lord, save me!'" (Psalm 116:4).

> "Everyone who calls on the name of the Lord
> will be saved" (Romans 10:13).

Review

This fourth *Reset* is also known as the u_____ *Reset*.

I receive and _____ Jesus as my personal S _____, and I now enjoy my relationship of _____ _____ _____ with _____ forever.

I am a _____ of God based on grace and f _____.

Reset #____

I now visualize God _____ down to personally _____ and _____ me when I _____ and _____ for his _____ and _____.

Reset # ____

I believe that God _____ , that his _____ is true, and that real _____ and _____ are my rewards for _____ him.
.

Reset # ____

I am on _____ mind _____ _____.

(even if I _____ _____ ___)

I really do _____ to God, and He is always _____ precious _____ about me.

Today, I ____ ____ _____ be on my _____ _____.

Continue reviewing and repeating each of the first four *Resets*, learning them word-for-word. Add the verses to memory as well. Receive and accept them as absolute truth from God and as foundations for your 28-day *reset* journey.

Here is a list of the supportive biblical verses from the New Living Translation that we have encountered so far in our journey.

Romans 12:2
Psalm 139:17
Hebrews 11:6
Psalm 86:1
Psalm 86:5
Psalm 116:4
Romans 10:13

Today's Prayer

O Lord,

The greatest rescue story I ever told will be my own personal spiritual rescue by Jesus Christ. I thank you, God, that you love me so much that you will forgive me of all the wrongs that I have ever done, all the mistakes that I have ever made, and all the sins I that I have ever committed against you and against other people. There is no greater cleansing of the heart and mind than simply accepting by faith what you have already accomplished for me through your son, Jesus, on the cross. All of my guilt, all of my shame, and all of the stain of my sins are washed away and removed by believing in Jesus and calling out His name to be saved. Please, Lord, save me! Renew and restore my relationship with you today. Amen.

Day 16

Everything Is Made Right with God Forever

If you confess with your mouth that Jesus is Lord and believe in your heart that God raised him from the dead, you will be saved. For it is by believing in your heart that you are made right with God, and it is by confessing with your mouth that you are saved. **Romans 10:9-10**

All of us handle difficult situations and personality conflicts differently. Personally, I do not like them at all, but I have learned that they are inevitable if I am going live with and be around other people on a daily basis. Much of the time, our conflicts and tensions with other people happen simply because people tend to confront and deal with issues differently, based on their natural personality variances. In marriages, most couples will discover this early in their marriage, if they did not recognize it before they fell in love and committed to each other. Some couples learn quickly how to resolve their differences during their early little skirmishes or even during their all-out-battles better than others do. Issues can build up in a marriage quietly over many months or years before they broil over into a heated conflict. On the other hand, they can suddenly come blazing around the corner without any ominous warning sirens going off. Some couples ignore the obvious danger signs and refuse to explore and consider the underlying issues that eventually germinate into full-blown conflicts. For them, it is much easier to pull the plug on the marriage and try another relationship, or two, or three! The problem with this run-and-hide escapism is that there are still a lot of similar pains waiting around the next corner in the next relationship for the slow learners who opt for this approach.

On other fronts, if all is well right now at home, then the workplace is the next best breeding ground for personality conflicts and disharmony to occur. If not there, then there are always the infamous church splits, or the nosey next-door neighbors, or the kids' teachers at school, or the other parents on the Saturday morning soccer field, or . . . the list goes on and on.

Alternatively, it is encouraging to be more positive and realize that even though all these conflicts and tensions are inevitable because of our humanity, they can be resolved with the right spirit, attitude, and effort by all parties in the particular relationships. Going back to our marriage illustration, there is probably nothing healthier for a marriage than the successful and productive resolution of a conflict. Bringing two very different people together, as a marriage does, and making them into one is no easy task. It takes time and much give-and-take effort on both spouses to become as one. Many older couples who have been married for several decades will acknowledge that they endured a few places in their journeys that could have ended by going separate ways. However, they chose to remember and honor their vows to each other, to revive and nurture their first love for one another, and to learn to enjoy each other's companionship on the journey despite their personality differences.

The point of this illustration of marriage reconciliation is to highlight the joys and the benefits of mending broken relationships whenever possible. This same joy and tension relief also occurs when feuding coworkers mend their relational fences at work. It happens when enraged parents and teenagers finally talk to each other and find a peaceful way to live together again. If we are all completely honest with ourselves, interpersonal conflicts make us miserable until they are finally resolved. Unfortunately, many conflicts are swept under the rug and never dealt with. Deep-seated issues like abuse and other family dysfunctional situations can be difficult to unwrap and deal with. However, when those issues and conflicts are effectively dealt with and when genuine healing and restoration eventually occurs, the individual and emotional freedom can be compared to heavy prison chains and shackles that have finally been unlocked and removed forever. It is truly being set free.

When restorations do take place in any of the situations mentioned above, we often hear that two people have patched up their differences and everything is now cool between them. A more accurate conclusion would be that they have made things right and have torn down the wall of hard feelings between them and replaced it with a vibrant and renewed friendship. In situations of complete reconciliation, it is as if the broken relationship had never occurred at all. Some objective observers might even say that their friendship or relationship is now stronger than ever.

Did You Know You Can Be Made
Right like That Again with God?

Many people unfortunately miss this key part of the Bible's primary message of restoration. They have heard the nutshell version of the gospel found in John 3:16 and hang on to it as a quick insurance to keep them out of hell and make it past heaven's entrance committee when they die. So in order to play the system, they just have to figure out how to save on a lifetime of "premiums" and only accept the deal and its heavenly benefits closer to the end of their lives. They say, "Why not? It has a guaranteed insurability clause. Just look right here! Everyone who believes in Him will not perish but have eternal life, and I really would like to live it up first and enjoy my life a little more while I'm here."

The ultimate *Reset* that we are currently considering on this journey is not an insurance policy that insures our entrance into God's heaven one day. It is much more than going to His kingdom (heaven) one day. Rather, it is about His kingdom coming to us and into our hearts and minds, changing us completely from the inside out. Yes, we who believe will joyfully one day be in God's heaven. However, in the meantime, God offers to fully repair, mend, and restore our broken and sin-marred relationships with Him. We can actually live out the rest of our lives here on the earth in the natural relationship with God that we were intended to enjoy all along. The Bible distinctly refers to this restored and reconciled relationship with Him as being made right with God. God freely grants to us a declared and undeserved state of "right being" in his eyes. It is also stated as being made righteous. But some people go another direction with this and imply that we somehow acquire this righteousness by our good deeds. Then we become good enough in God's eyes and strive even more in our good deeds for spiritual perfection. However, we should remember from our journey so far, "good people don't go to heaven, forgiven people go to heaven."

To understand the clear difference, it may help to hear it this way: "Right being" outranks "right doing" every time! The gospel truth is much easier to understand if we just listen and hear what God's Word actually says, not how some religious groups misinterpret and present it.

> **"For it is by believing in your heart that you
> are made right with God . . ." (Romans 10:10).**

Your ultimate *reset* happens in your life when you choose to believe in your heart that God has done His part to restore your relationship with Him, and when you receive and embrace your newly declared state of being made right with God (or being righteous in His sight). What other people conclude about you makes no difference. They may know your past all too well and point out your faults and weaknesses and mistakes, but your new status has completely wiped away the past, and He remembers it no more! He has decisively dealt with your end of the spiritual conflict so that you now bear no more guilt. God restores your relationship with Him, and you can fully reclaim and start living the life that you should be living. Now that is why we call this part of our 28-day journey, the ultimate *Reset*! There is more to complete in this *reset* journey, but this is the key one. No other healing of a broken relationship in life compares to the restoration of your friendship with God. This new relationship with Him is the most wonderful and liberating fresh start that you will ever experience this side of heaven.

There Is Nothing like Having Your Heart in Sync with God's!

About the time I was writing down some initial thoughts and outlines for this book, I started having some physical heart issues. I have always exercised and stayed active. I was healthy, and other than some mild hypertension, had no serious heart conditions. Gradually though, I began to notice some slight aberrations in my heartbeat, accompanied by occasional light-headedness, mild shortness of breath, and periods of general tiredness. Over a period of several months, my cardiologist and his nurse carefully monitored the increasing frequency and duration of my episodes. What started out as brief and sporadic moments of rapid heartbeats and skips, punctuated by unnerving pauses for several seconds, became more frequent and symptomatic. The episodes of palpitations would last anywhere from five minutes to sometimes over twelve hours.

Eventually, we caught the pattern of the cardiac arrhythmias on an EKG monitor. It was determined that I was experiencing atrial flutters and atrial fibrillations. In other words, the electrical functions of my heart were abnormally misfiring in the upper atrial chamber, creating the erratic heartbeat patterns. At least when I woke up at night experiencing an irregular heartbeat episode, I knew I wasn't having a heart attack. The downside to this condition was that I did run the slight risk of a possible blood clot forming in the heart and creating a stroke condition.

My cardiologist referred me to a cardiac electrophysiologist, who quickly determined that I was a good candidate for a procedure called a cardiac catheter ablation, which would pinpoint the sources and location of my electrical misfires and then destroy those areas of tissue. An ablation procedure is usually quite successful. Utilizing three catheter sites and a transesophageal echocardiogram, my entire ablation took seven hours. My procedure went well, and so far, the arrhythmia symptoms have not returned.

The reason I share that story is simple. Today, I feel so much better than when my heart was all out of sync with its normal heartbeat pattern. My erratic symptoms were strong enough to cause concern and to seek the advice and help of a specialist. Prior to his intervention and the longer my heart stayed out of sync, the more miserable I felt. In my case, the diagnosis was clear and the corrective procedure was available and successful. The way I look at it now, the heart specialist performed a *reset* on my physical heart, and now that my heart is once again beating properly, I am enjoying the life that I, a healthy person my age, should be living.

Can you see where this is going? When sin in our lives interferes and disrupts the proper relationship that we should be having with God, our spiritual hearts are out of sync with Him. The symptoms and results of this broken relationship vary in degree and intensity from person to person. However, the result of this untreated spiritual condition is always the same: separation from God, both now in this life and eternally in the next life!

God is the heart specialist in this situation and has the only effective procedure to examine our hearts, to pinpoint where the problem areas of sin are, and to apply the redemptive work of Jesus Christ to get our spiritual relationships back in sync with Him. The choice in this ultimate *reset* for you and me is to stay in our sinfulness and stay out of step with God, or to choose to call out to God and ask Him to save us and restore our rightful relationships with Him through Jesus. I hope you can see that there is nothing better than having your heart in sync once again with God's heart.

If you have never done so, you can make the choice today to call out to God and become right with Him. By putting it off, you only delay and might even miss forever the ultimate *reset* that can give you your own fresh start in life. Simply receive and embrace Jesus as your personal Savior, and you will enjoy your relationship of being made right with God forever.

If you are already a Christian and have previously made this choice, use this opportunity to pause and reflect on the unmerited and undeserved goodness of God in your life. Thank Him again for His previous specialist work in your heart where, like a precision laser, He pinpointed the specific needs of your heart, removed your sins, and restored your relationship with Him forever.

* * *

Here again is the verse that we quoted at the beginning of today's chapter. As a bonus verse for *Reset #4*, write it below the first two supportive verses on your fourth card.

"If you confess with your mouth that Jesus is Lord and believe in your heart that God raised him from the dead, you will be saved. For it is by believing in your heart that you are made right with God, and it is by confessing with your mouth that you are saved" (Romans 10:9-10).

Review

You are now past the halfway point on your 28-day journey. Reviewing and learning each *Reset* self-talk statement word-for-word is your primary task each day. These statements are carefully worded in such a way as to be faithful to what God says in His Word. By repeatedly stating them, you internalize them and soon they become your own words. By now, you know how words can powerfully change the input going into your mind and heart. When you internalize each statement and personally begin to believe and embrace them, your core beliefs will begin to change during this 28-day *reset* journey. Then of course, your attitudes, followed by your feelings, will start to change. After that, your feelings will start affecting some of your daily actions or behaviors. Because of this *reset* process, you will begin to notice significant changes in the net results of your life. The simplicity of *The Reset* journey is that consistent changes in your input will change the output in your life. In other words, living differently begins with thinking differently. The beauty of this approach is that the authority and power of these biblically based self-talk statements come from the reliable truth of God's Word. All of the *Resets* are key ones, yet *Reset #4* is the ultimate one because the focus is on you personally being made right with God by receiving and embracing Jesus as your personal Savior. Fill in the blanks below for this *Reset* and then spend some time where needed reviewing your previous statements and verses.

I receive and _____ Jesus as ____ _____ _____.
and I now enjoy my _____ of being ____
right with _____ _____.

I am a _____ __ _____ based on _____ and
_____.

"Then I called on the _____ of the _____: 'Please, _____,
_____ __ '" Psalm 116:____.

"Everyone who _____ on the _____ __ ____ _____ will be
_____" Romans ____:13.

Today's Prayer

Dear God,

One of life's biggest challenges in our frantic, busy world today is getting along with other people. I know that some conflicts are going to happen, but it still makes me wish that they did not. It is encouraging though when two individuals or two groups of people can come together to resolve their differences and restore their friendships. Too often we are tempted to run and hide when things get a little tense and never give our broken relationships a chance to be healed and restored. Today I want to focus on my relationship with you, God. If there is some brokenness or weak spots in my relationship with you, help me to see and acknowledge it. If I need to be made right with you today, O Lord, let me follow the example in Romans 10:9-10. On the other hand, if there is something else coming between us, speak to me with your inner voice and point that issue out to me so that I can face it and deal with it right now. My deepest core need will always be the ongoing spiritual condition of my heart, so Lord, be my heart specialist today and make sure that you mend any brokenness in our relationship. I give you permission to do that! Amen.

Day 17

You Are a Friend of God

So now we can rejoice in our wonderful new relationship with God because our Lord Jesus Christ has made us friends of God. **Romans 5:11**

A recent contemporary Christian song reminds every believer in Jesus that he or she is a friend of God. The lyrics of that song tell us that God is thinking of us, that He hears us when we when call out to Him, and that God considers us His friend! In the verse quoted above, it is also obvious from Paul's letter to the church at Rome that he understood when we are made right with God, we enter into a whole new intimate level of friendship with Him.

Even though Romans 5:11 has been right there in the Bible all along, for some reason, many people must have skipped right over its implications. I can only assume for them that maybe their focus has been so much on following religious rules and rigorous church expectations that, most of the time, they have not been able to enjoy their wonderful freedom in Christ and the benefits of a real day-to-day, intimate friendship with God.

Going back to Genesis, the first book in the Bible, we recall that when God created the first man and woman, Adam and Eve, He enjoyed an unbroken, intimate fellowship with them. However, sin marred that close fellowship with Adam and Eve and for all future generations when they gave in to sin's temptation and disobeyed God. That is where the term *original sin* comes from. Since that first sin, everyone born into this world has inherited the tendency to sin or disobey God. From early childhood on, we grow up preferring to do things our own ways. Any parent of young children that you ask will tell you just how strong this self-will tendency is!

Just like Adam and Eve, as we grow older in life, we tend to question God's guidelines for living and would rather follow the crowd and live only to please ourselves rather than live to please God. The longer we do this and turn our backs on God, the greater our separation between Him and us grows. As this separation continues, it becomes easier to do what is wrong and harder to do what is actually right. After a while, we lose much of our ability to know the clear difference between right and wrong.

As the years go by, the wisdom of the world guides our lifestyles more than the wisdom of God, and we continue to reap what we sow, whether it is good or bad. That law of the universe will never change and will always be a big part of the story of our lives.

Who Are You Going to Choose to Run or Hang With?

As a young boy growing up, I remember that many adult figures in my life would remind me that it was important to consider the type of kids that I was running around with. Today's parents would perhaps say, "Be careful who you are hanging around with." In other words, they are encouraging their kids to choose their close friends carefully. I think all of us would agree that is great advice for life, but somehow we don't always apply the same principle very well in our own lives.

Think for a moment about some of the times that you have personally made some terrible mistakes or poor decisions in your life. Did you end up reaping what you sowed? How many times did a friend partially influence you in a negative way to do what you did? What might have been different had your choice of friends been different in that situation? I am not saying that we should blame our friends for all of our bad choices or actions in life. What we do is our responsibility! However, true friends do hold each other to a higher standard and help each other make good choices as they navigate through life together. Furthermore, real friends give us many other positive benefits that we cannot put a price tag on.

As we wrap up *Reset* #4 today, I want to try to make this idea of friendship with God something real, but at the same time, not take away from the primary and urgent need to first be made right with God. Friendship with God only comes after we receive and embrace Jesus as our personal Savior. Let's look again at what Paul says in Romans 5:11. "So now we can rejoice in our wonderful new relationship with God because our Lord Jesus Christ has made us friends of God."

What does this mean for you on this 28-day *reset* journey? Think about it. You have the privilege of hanging out with God every day for the rest of your life! Without taking advantage of the ultimate *reset* in your life, you will miss out on the most incredible friendship ever. God's grace and forgiveness is the total basis for this friendship. Through Jesus, God has broken down the wall of separation that sin had erected between you and Him. If you confess with your mouth and believe in your heart, then God will forgive you of all your sins, and He will restore the broken friendship with Him that you were originally created to enjoy. It is impossible for me to put into words an adequate description of what an intimate friendship with God is like, but let me share a few things that a new member of my household has taught me recently about what my relationship with God can be like.

Abby, Six Pounds of Unconditional Love, Trust, and Friendship

Many studies have shown the emotional friendship and other physical and mental benefits household pets often bring into our lives. In my entire lifetime, I have probably had at least ten dogs or cats. Each of them held a special place in my heart and was unique in its own way. I have had dogs of all sizes, cats of various fur lengths and colors, a couple of parakeets, and even a few goldfish. I will admit though that I get more attached to my dogs! Let me give you a highlight of a few of my dogs.

Benji was my little white Westie who was full of personality and energy. He was our first "child" since it took my wife and I a while to start our family. I remember seeing the classified ad in the newspaper and driving over two hours to Charlotte, North Carolina, to get him and bring him home. As a puppy, he was so little, but his heart was so big! Several years later after my sons were born, Jonathan and Jeremiah loved their energetic little playmate, and it was so much fun watching the three of them run and play in our backyard. Benji had some favorite indoor tricks that he did with a tennis ball, but outside, he loved to fetch a slightly deflated volleyball and bring it back in his little mouth. The ball was much bigger than his whole head, so it totally obscured his vision as he carried it. Furthermore, his legs were short and sometimes when he lost his grip on the volleyball, he would temporarily drop it and his unthrottled forward momentum would shoot his little belly and legs right over the top of the ball. Even though we would all get a great laugh out of it, Benji never thought we were laughing at him. He just thought he was providing us with a pleasurable moment, which he was! It still deeply hurts us today to recall the unexpected day that we were not able to bring him back home with us from the veterinarian's office. A severe kidney complication rudely interrupted our ten years of unconditional canine love and friendship with Benji. Our boys were in elementary school at the time when we had to break the sad news to them.

With our hearts so torn, we tried as a family to vow that we would not get another dog. Then after a short while, a friend called and told us about a little "rescue" puppy that we might like to see. I hesitantly asked my friend what kind of dog it was. He said with a little suspicion in his voice that it was just a cute little black dog. He was withholding some major truth. Even though this dog was about eight months old, not yet fully grown, she already weighed about forty pounds. Despite our friend's lack of full disclosure, we eventually gave in and Mollie became our next dog, a beautiful black lab. Apparently, someone found her as an older puppy in Colorado Springs, Colorado, during a severe thunderstorm. She was tethered unmercifully to a utility pole, soaking wet, and terrified from the many lighting strikes. Mollie eventually became a great dog even though it was evident that she had suffered some earlier abuse by someone. At that time, I was jogging quite a bit, so Mollie became my faithful running partner and friend. She also accompanied our adventurous family on many mountain hiking excursions on the trails in the Pikes Peak area. Mollie lived a long dog's life and moved three times with our family to new locations. She was sixteen when she finally could not go any further. I often sensed that Mollie was only giving us about 75 percent of her natural friendship because her early abuse must have been so traumatic. But that 75 percent that she did give was so much fun! Our boys were out of college and on to newer phases of their own lives when we had to break the news to them.

This time, my wife and I decided that since we like to travel away from home several times a year, we would definitely not get another dog. This time we were firm with our decision and in complete partnership agreement. I don't know what got into me, but I have to confess here, it was all my fault! I caved in rather quickly and spent one night searching the Internet for my next puppy. I am not a politician, but it was a good flip-flop on my part! My wife objected only a little at first, and then she too caved in. Within two days, we were captured prisoners, desperately torn between our choices of two precious little Shih Tzu puppies. It was such an agonizing choice that after several hours, we almost brought both of them home. We finally did make our choice and brought home the most precious and loveable three pounds of puppy that you could ever find. Both of our sons could not believe the text pictures of Abby that I proudly sent them that evening. Within seconds, I fielded surprised cell phone calls from both of them questioning, "What have you done now?"

Abby has become the most loving little dog-friend that my wife and I have ever had. She now weighs a whopping six pounds, but daily this little Shih Tzu takes our hearts down with her unconditional love, trust, and friendship. It is hard to imagine a day without her, but we have continued to take our trips away from home, only because Abby has a second home next door with our neighbors, Bill and Ellen.

Let me tell you a little more about my relationship with Abby. When we first brought her home as a puppy, I was her primary teacher and trainer. Housebreaking went well, and soon we moved on to more advanced learning. Abby, or Abigail, as I sometimes affectionately call her, had an insatiable desire from our first night together to be close to me and to start learning some tricks. She also seemed to enjoy doing little things that would please me. The more she responded to me, the more I would also take great delight in her.

You probably know where this is going. Abby has become like a best friend, one who you really want to be around, one who gives you unconditional love and trust all the time, and one who brings overall great pleasure and value to your life.

Today, Abby wants to be with me wherever I am in our home. For instance, when I am sitting in my recliner and writing this book on my laptop, she is either nestled between the armrest and my left thigh, or she is perched like a parrot, lying with all six pounds distributed evenly between my neck and the back of the recliner. Every once in a while she will give me a wet "sugar kiss" with her tongue on my ear lobe or cheek, as if she is encouraging me to keep on writing and finish the current chapter. She only interrupts me when she occasionally needs her outside break. That is when she will get down and go ring her potty bell to go outside for a walk. Other times, she just wants me to throw one of her squeaky toys for her to fetch. If I go to play the piano for a few minutes, she has to sit on the bench beside my right thigh. When I go to sit in my massage chair, she wants to be in my lap to feel every massage cycle and every muscle vibration with me. When I go to my outside patio to read, to relax, or to eat a snack in my two-seater swing, yes, she wants to be right by my side, enjoying the sounds of the birds and the occasional plane overhead. Even when I carry out the garbage, she will run and perch herself on the back of our chaise chair and maintain her stakeout of my movements until I come back inside. What am I saying here? Abby simply loves to be with me!

She also likes to bring pleasure to me. She loves to do her tricks and entertain any guests we may have. She likes to sit, to lie down, to roll over, to turn around, to shake hands, to give a high five, to stand, and to dance. But her favorite trick of all is to work on her suntan. She will flop over on her back and spread all of her paws out as if she is at the beach on her favorite beach towel. It is so funny when I bring out a treat and simply ask her what she can do. She immediately plunges into a quickly thrown together routine, combining several tricks into one hilarious act, but throwing in her infamous suntan trick as a grand finale. She somehow knows that she is bringing laughter and great pleasure to her audience.

For my part, I enjoy being with Abby too. I love on her. I take care of her daily needs. I speak good words to her all the time. In short, I take great delight in her and love on her a lot. In return, she takes great delight in me and loves on me and anyone else who is around. Abby is a full whopping six pounds of unconditional love, trust, and friendship in the Stevens' home.

Your Everyday Friendship with God Should Be like That!

When you choose to *reset* your relationship to God by receiving and embracing Jesus as your personal Savior, you will begin to experience a new friendship with God, completely based on grace and forgiveness. As we have emphasized earlier, you will never be good enough to merit God's friendship. Only God's forgiveness can make you right with Him. You then become a friend of God as the Bible so truthfully declares.

Mutual trust and unconditional love are the basis for all true friendships. It is no different with God. Your new friendship with God will grow over time to be better than any earthly friendship could ever be. You will increasingly want to be with God and go wherever He goes. You will discover what pleases your heavenly Father and have a greater desire to do those things, even as Jesus, our perfect example, did in the Bible. Moreover, as God takes great delight in you, you will likewise take great delight in Him!

To conclude this ultimate *Reset*, look again at Romans 10:9-10 and focus on the key word, *confess*. It is this self-talk that comes out of your mouth by faith that saves you from your sinfulness and makes you right with God.

"If you confess with your mouth that Jesus is Lord and believe in your heart that God raised him from the dead, you will be saved. For it is by believing in your heart that you are made right with God, and it is by confessing with your mouth that you are saved."

Receiving and embracing Jesus is the ultimate *reset* for your life. Just believe and accept by faith your new relationship with God through Jesus. If you have already become a Christian at some point earlier in your life, use this *Reset* to renew your relationship with God and continue receiving and embracing Jesus as your personal Savior every day from now on. If you come to Him, He will certainly come to you. Now that is good news!

Review

We call our fourth *Reset* the _____ _____. All the other *Resets* on our journey are important, but this one is the central one!

I _____ and _____ Jesus as my _____ _____, and I now enjoy __ _____ of _____ _____ _____ with _____ _____.

I am a _____ ___ _____ based on grace and _____.

124

Use the space below to write out the first three *Resets*, and then use your cards to review the Bible verses that support each of your first four self-talk statements.

Reset #1

_____

_____

_____

_____

_____

Reset #2

_____

_____

_____

_____

_____

Reset #3

_____

_____

_____

_____

_____

Today's Prayer

Dear heavenly Father,

This 28-day journey has been a wonderful breath of fresh air for my life, and now to know you as a friend is life changing for me. Thank you for allowing Jesus to tear down the wall of separation that my sin had built up between us. Wow, I never knew that this *reset* journey was going to transform my life by changing the way I think. O God, there are still so many things that I need help with in my life, so please be patient with me as I learn to walk with you. Help me to be patient with myself and to take one day at a time. When I mess up, help me to remember that I am still on your mind and you still think precious thoughts about me. Remind me to believe in you and to rely on the truth of your Word as I change the way I think. I am the gatekeeper of my thoughts. I can pray and visualize you personally bending down to hear and answer me when I pray and ask for your help and guidance. Help me memorize each *Reset* self-talk statement and the verses that support them. Again, thank you for giving me a fresh start! Amen.

RESET #5

Day 18

It's Time to Be Bold and Draw Your Line in the Sand

Guard your heart above all else,
for it determines the course of your life. **Proverbs 4:23**

We were living in the Phoenix, Arizona, area at one time when a thief broke into our home in broad daylight. Our twin boys were in kindergarten at the time, but on this particular day, they were not in school. My parents had never been to Phoenix, so they flew out from North Carolina to visit with us for a few days. We wanted to show them around and planned a full day to drive around the city and see some of the main highlights. We started early in the morning and finished our tour late in the afternoon. We were hot and exhausted when we finally pulled back into our subdivision. I think we all just wanted to get inside and rest our feet a bit while the boys were probably thinking about a cool swim in the backyard pool. As we rounded the corner, our home was just a few houses down the road. I'll never forget the sick feeling that instantaneously invaded my stomach when we saw the police car in our driveway and the officer standing inside the foyer of our open front door.

After some quick formal introductions with each other and once the officer could conclude that we were the rightful occupants of the house, we approached the house and could see where the front door had been kicked open with aggressive force. Broken glass was lying everywhere, and another officer inside was taking notes on a pad and writing up a preliminary report. He then informed us that a neighbor across the street had initially noticed the shattered front door and had called the police to report a possible break in. There had been a string of such burglaries occurring recently in the neighborhood, so everyone was sort of on high alert status to anything looking suspicious.

The officers allowed us to scan the house to do an initial inventory and report any missing items. The first thing that we wanted to find was Benji, our little West Highland White Terrier that I mentioned earlier. Fortunately, our perpetrator had decided not to hurt Benji and had simply opened the sliding glass door to the back yard to let him out, probably to just stop his barking. Other than being extremely hot and thirsty, Benji was fine. We only wish he could talk and tell us what had happened and who had been in our home.

Our inventory of missing items suggested a quick break-in. It was apparent that our uninvited intruder was looking for items that could be pawned for some quick cash. I think he got our VCR, some jewelry, a cheap camera, and a few other items that I can't even remember now. Having some personal items stolen was bad enough, but what really made us angry was the fact that, in his haste, he pulled open every single dresser and cabinet drawer, rummaged indiscriminately through my parents' luggage, most of our personal items and clothing, and made a general disarray of our whole house!

Whoever had broken into our home had violated our personal space, had disregarded all of our personal rights, and had injected a shadowy-like fear into our minds that would last for days. *This thief, whoever he was, had no right whatsoever breaking into my house and doing his evil mischief.* I was outraged to say the least! At that moment, I have to admit that the thought passed briefly through my mind that I wished I had stationed a few attack dogs in my house before I had left that morning. I would much rather have come home and found a dog like that lying at my front door chewing on the perpetrator's kicking shoe and half of his torn pants leg! I am sure that Benji had put no fear into him and had only barked because he wanted to play fetch with his tennis ball. I know that my impromptu thought was just a passing fantasy of revenge, but I still remember it to this day, and it leads me into introducing our newest *Reset* self-talk statement today. We will spend the next few days unfolding it and explaining its importance for your *reset* journey. If you have already experienced the ultimate *reset* of receiving and embracing Jesus as your personal Savior, and I hope you have, then this *Reset* is where you must be strong and make another choice to draw your line in the sand. The enemy will not give up easily, and he will fight hard to convince you that you are making a big mistake. He is the same lying enemy that Adam and Eve faced in the garden.

Here is *Reset* #5, so take a moment now and write it out on an index card. Be sure to underline the words *diligently guard my heart*.

~~~~~~

Reset #5

I *diligently guard my heart* to keep it ready to receive God's overflowing grace and mercy, which are brand new to me every single day.

This enables me to rest peacefully in God's goodness and to walk daily in His presence.

Now, on the back of your card, write this Bible verse at the top. Leave room at the bottom for two more short verses that we will add later.

"Guard your heart above all else, for it determines the course of your life" (Proverbs 4:23).

~~~~~~

Do You Understand What Is at Stake?

In order for you to reclaim the life you should be living during this 28-day *reset* journey, you must understand what is at stake. Once you understand what the real battle is all about, then you will have to be willing to draw your line in the sand and to take a stand. On Day 5 of this journey, we shared how we all love rescue stories. For some reason, we love it when the good guy comes up on the scene and places himself right into the dangerous battle to stare down the bad guy eye-to-eye. By showing up, he takes a bold stand for what is right and draws a line in the sand. By his bold action, he declares in that moment, "Right is right, even if everyone is against it; and wrong is wrong, even if everyone is for it."

131

In warfare, when the victor of a battle makes a surge and lays claim to occupy a newly captured territory, he must first take steps to secure the territory, and then he must implement a strategy to guard and protect the territory from a possible counter attack. The victor must always be aware of the potential that the enemy may at some point try to come back and retake his lost territory. In spiritual terms, if you recently received and embraced Jesus as your personal Savior, your enemy, Satan, lost his territory in your life. He realizes that Jesus has won the battle for your eternal soul, but that does not mean that he is going to give up and not try to sabotage your new life in Christ.

Knowing the Battle Over Our Hearts and Minds

John 10:10 perfectly lays this epic battle out for us to see. This is what is on the line and what Jesus actually said about it. You will find additions emphasis in brackets. "The thief's [Satan's] purpose is to steal and kill and destroy. My [Jesus's] purpose is to give them a rich and satisfying life." We shared with you on Day 9 about real joy and strength being a part of the rewards of God. In addition to that, God blesses us every single day with his never-ending faithfulness and lavishly pours out new grace and mercy on us. To counter that blessed life, Satan still "roams like a lion," trying to devour the fruit of God's blessings in our lives.

Reset #5 is so important because it reminds us each day that we must diligently guard the reclaimed territory of our hearts that Jesus now owns and occupies. When we post a 24/7 guard on our hearts, it is both an offensive position and a defensive position. The new life that we now have in Christ is a valuable treasure deposited in our hearts. It is like a planted seed that if carefully nurtured, will germinate and grow and mature. It gradually begins to produce more and more of the fruits of the Spirit in our lives (Galatians 5:22-23). As it continues to mature, it transforms us through and through, and our character begins to reflect the image of Christ. However, even though Satan has already lost the eternal battle at the cross, he still rules over the evil powers in this world order temporarily until the last day when Christ returns and Satan's final doom is sealed. Until then, the only thing that Satan can do is to attempt to steal, kill, and destroy that valuable treasure that is rightfully ours in Christ. Be warned. He will try to sabotage your life too.

God sent Jesus to defeat Satan and to take back the territory of our hearts and minds. We know that Jesus completed His part of God's mission, but He also equipped us with the awareness and the supernatural power of His Spirit to both offensively and defensively guard our hearts against Satan's counter attacks.

Offensively, you and I must be proactive and go on the attack when necessary to protect and guard the treasure of the gospel, or the good news of Christ, in our hearts. This means that we live daily in such a way as to proactively thwart ahead of time (as the Secret Service does for a traveling president) any possible avenues of attack that Satan might use against us. We will all face various trials and temptations, but we all personally know what our greatest weaknesses are and where the likely attacks might come from. As men and women, we will also have some gender-specific temptations that are obvious, and we would be wise to be ahead of the game in those critical areas. Know what your response and reaction will be when those situations arise. Realize that the real source behind the attack might be Satan coming around to steal, kill, or destroy something in your life or your family. If you offensively draw the line in the sand here with this *Reset*, then the daily battles will be easier to fight, your responses will be quick and decisive, and your heart will always be ready to receive God's fresh, overflowing grace and mercy, which are brand new every single day.

Defensively, Ephesians 6 shows us a great word picture of the spiritual armor that is available to defend the territory of our hearts and minds. One of those primary pieces is described as the sword of the Spirit, which is the Word of God. That is why we support each of our *Reset* statements with specific Scriptures and why you should memorize these verses. I can think of no better weapon to carry with you than a memorized portion of Scripture that you can recall and quote at a moment's notice. Satan cannot stand against the Word of God. However, you must bear your weapon faithfully and not let it rust from lack of use. A sword undrawn in these spiritual battles is useless.

Is Your Heart's Security System Installed and Operating?

Do you remember how angry our family felt when the thief invaded and compromised our home, which was supposedly our safe, personal territory? Rummaging around through my stuff and stealing what was not his made me mad. If you have ever had something stolen from you, you know the feeling. If you can relate to a home robbery, then you should have that same anger toward your spiritual enemy who comes to steal, kill, and destroy the sacred treasure deposited in your heart. I firmly believe that most of our defeats and setbacks in life come because we do not diligently guard our hearts. When we neglect guarding our hearts, we compromise the readiness and receptivity of our hearts for the good things of God. I am convinced that most of us, even Christians, miss much of the overflowing grace and mercy that flows to us from God on a daily basis. Grace and mercy are right there in front of us, ever flowing like a mighty river, but our hearts are not ready to receive them.

Make the choice today to allow *Reset* #5 to transform your life by continuing to change the way you think. Draw your line in the sand today. I cannot say it any better than this.

"Guard you heart above all else, for it determines the course of your life."

Review

Focus today only on the first part of our new *Reset* statement. Go back and review your card for a few minutes. Focus on each word. Say it aloud to yourself at least ten times. Pause for a few moments and let this one really sink in. Then picture yourself proactively drawing your line in the sand and declaring that you will defend and guard your heart and mind. No one will successfully steal, kill, or destroy what God has graciously given to you in Jesus!

Now fill in the blanks below.

I _____ _____ my heart to keep it _____ to receive God's overflowing g_____ and m_____, which are brand _____ to me every single ____.

"Guard your _____ above ____ ____, for it determines the course of your ____" Proverbs 4:____.

As part of your daily review, continue each day to say aloud each *Reset* statement that we have given so far on this journey. You will have to determine how many times you need to do this each day.

Please don't skip this important daily part of your *reset* journey! I want you to know each *Reset* word-for-word without hesitation at the end of our journey. The verses are equally important, but give them second priority for now if you need extra time on the *Resets*. I have always found it helpful to pull my cards out several different times during the day and review them often. Then I like to review them one last time before going to bed at night. If you ever miss a day's reading, don't panic. Just pick up where you left off the next day and stick with reading only one chapter a day. If the journey is a little fast paced for your style, then slow down and maybe do a new chapter every two days. However, still do your daily review of your cards.

Again, let me say how happy I am that you are taking this journey with me to reclaim the life you should be living! God is so good, and I want you to enjoy His faithfulness and friendship every single day.

Today's Prayer

O God, who restores my life,

I think back to the first day of this *reset* journey and being encouraged to focus my thoughts on letting you transform me into a new person by changing the way I think. I was definitely in need of a fresh start, and I wanted to check it out. With the help of the *Reset* statements, I find myself thinking differently now about some key areas of my life, and I am enjoying my growing relationship with you each day. Some of my old ways of thinking are still changing a little slowly, but I am seeing progress. Negative thoughts from my past that have affected my life are becoming easier to let go of, and I am learning to replace them with thoughts based on your encouraging words to me from the Bible. It is easier now for me to pray and just talk to you about my life. You have set me free from my past sins. I am saved and I am now a friend of yours all because of your grace and forgiveness! Jesus is now my Savior, whom I receive and embrace every day. O God, I want to guard my heart and my mind diligently. Help me to be a more faithful gatekeeper, because I do not want to miss any of the overflowing grace and mercy that you send my way each day. Amen.

Day 19

The Receptivity of Your Heart
Is a Key Vital Sign

During the year that I was dealing with the abnormal and erratic heartbeats, I made several visits a month to my cardiologist's office. Some of those doctor's visits were routine checkups as we tried to determine why I was having so many unusual heart issues and symptoms, considering my age and previously good health. Even my blood pressure was being stubborn and hard to regulate. My doctor ordered many different kinds of tests to find a medical solution over a period of several months. It was one attempt after another to find the underlying cause of my medical condition. He tested my blood, hooked me up to a variety of machines, scanned different parts of my body, made me wear monitors for weeks at a time, and adjusted the dosages of my medicines. In other words, he methodically tested all of my vital signs to focus on the cause of my abnormal heart symptoms.

We got lucky one afternoon and finally got a definitive EKG while my heart was having a crazy erratic heartbeat of its own for several hours. After reviewing this particular EKG, it was determined that I was experiencing atrial flutters and atrial fibrillation. My cardiologist helped me immensely when he explained what was happening and that I needed to see another kind of heart specialist. He said, "When it comes to treating your heart, I am like a plumber. I try to regulate the flow of blood through your heart and out through your arteries and veins. I am going to refer you a doctor who will be like an electrician for your heart. You are a good candidate for a procedure called an ablation, which has a good success rate in correcting abnormal heart rhythms."

I am the type of person who likes that kind of frankness from my doctor. I want to do whatever it takes to find out what I am dealing with, go over my treatment options, and then proceed with a recommended plan of action to deal with the situation. From there I can move forward, trusting that God is in full control of the outcome.

In my case, the diagnosis concluded that my key vital signs pointed to an issue with the electrical impulses acting erratically and disrupting the normal rhythm of my heart.

Your Spiritual Heart Needs Regular Checkups Too

There is also a key vital sign that determines your heart's spiritual condition. When it comes to reclaiming the life that God wants you to enjoy, it initially starts by faith with the forgiveness of your sins when you receive and embrace Jesus Christ (*Reset #4*). When you are forgiven from your sins, your heart (the center or core of your being) experiences a cleansing that, in biblical terms, means you are spiritually born again. You become a new creation in the sense that you are once again living in an unbroken relationship with God the Father. This occurs when you make a willful decision to accept God's incredible offer that we talked about earlier on our journey.

After you make that initial choice and as you continue down life's road, your life should take on more of the characteristics of a life led by God. You were once susceptible to the negative influences and customs of a world dominated by the evil one, and you made most of your daily choices from that worldview. Now you have turned away from that pattern of living. You now make your daily choices from a worldview dominated more and more by your new relationship with God.

After the Gospels, much of the New Testament is a variety of letters written to general groups of new believers at large or to specific churches planted in various cities throughout the region at that time. Early church leaders wrote much of the content of those letters as spiritual heart checkups. The letters helped the early believers by encouraging them in their faith, by giving them helpful instruction on living a life pleasing to God, and by giving them appropriate warnings concerning things that could cause serious setbacks in their new relationship with God and with each other.

As you read the New Testament letters, notice the amount of space dedicated to helping Christian believers maintain their right relationship with God. Your own personal study of those letters will provide much more depth and knowledge in protecting and nurturing your faith. For our purposes here, I want to keep things simple and have you to focus your thoughts again on the first part of *Reset #5*.

> I diligently guard my heart to keep it ready to receive God's overflowing grace and mercy, which are brand new to me every single day.

Now that you understand that Christ has already won the final victory over Satan, you also know from John 10:10 that, in the meantime, Satan now has only one basic strategy. Satan wants to sabotage God's life in you. He will throw everything he can at you to steal, kill, or destroy the new life that Christ planted as a seed in your heart. Since God knows that you will face an ongoing battle for the territory of your heart and mind, He has warned you to guard this territory. I like to think of it as if God wants you to keep this territory under close surveillance to insure its safety and security. If you can successfully guard your heart, then there will be no compromises to interfere with receiving God's daily portions of new grace and mercy into your life.

The critical vital sign that I mentioned earlier is *the receptivity of your heart*. If you allow sin to infiltrate back into any of the areas of your heart, then your life will be spiritually compromised at that point. When that occurs, sin's infiltration will hinder the receptivity of your heart to God's faithful daily provisions.

All of us are encouraged by Scripture to examine our hearts and do a quick check to see if there is any sin present. If sin is present, then we must take corrective action to restore our heart's receptivity to God's grace and mercy. The Bible gives us the remedy to follow under such circumstances when sin is present. "If we confess our sins to him, he is faithful and just to forgive us our sins and to cleanse us from all wickedness." (1 John 1:9). Our hearts are then once again spiritually clean. A pure heart is one without the presence of sin, and a pure heart is the ideal spiritual condition for a believer to be perpetually ready to receive God's daily portions of grace and mercy. When we live every day with *a ready heart,* His blessings will flow in the spiritual realm to us like a steady, refreshing, overflowing river!

I have been river rafting or canoeing a few times in my life. It can be a great experience or it can be a miserable experience, depending on the amount of water flowing in the river. You definitely don't want to be dragging the bottom! That will take the joy right out of your day on the river for sure. Spiritually, we don't want to be dragging bottom either. If you and I will be diligent in guarding the territory of our hearts and minds, then God's overflowing river will be our daily expectation and enjoyment, no matter what circumstances life throws at us. When we cooperate with God and do our part to guard our hearts above all else, then the right course for our lives is determined on a day-by-day basis. Satan's efforts to sabotage us is effectively turned back daily by our diligent guard over our hearts.

Your Spiritual Supply Will Never Run Out

God's provisions flow to us daily. I think many Christians live hoping that their once-a-week church attendance will provide a whole week's worth of spiritual nourishment. If they experience an awesome worship service on the weekend, then they try to ride that spiritual high for the entire week. Spiritually and physically, we are designed for daily consumption. In the Lord's Prayer, we are encouraged to pray for daily bread, and for commonsense reasons, we do many other things on a daily basis, such as brush our teeth, take showers, and sleep at night. So start every day knowing that you will be relying on God's faithful provisions throughout that day. Keep your heart ready so that whenever God sends those blessings, you will have a high degree of heart receptivity and not miss His overflowing river that is passing your way.

As You Sit at His Table, Ask Him to Fill Your Cup

It is sad, but in our frantic paces of life, most people today forget to pause and thank God for the food that they eat at mealtimes. If that description fits you, I hope you will reconsider and start giving thanks for your food again. It will also be a good time to ask God to fill your spiritual cup and thank Him when He does. An old church song, "Fill My Cup, Lord," used to encourage this. The words of that song ask God to fill our lifted cups and to quench the thirsting in our souls. The lyrics go on to request that God would feed us His bread of heaven until we would want no more. What a great word picture of God as your daily source of all that you will ever need. He gives just what you need, just when you need it, and just enough to fill and satisfy your soul for that day's journey. Tomorrow's provision will faithfully come your way tomorrow. Therefore, your challenge for this *reset* journey is to thank God for His overflowing grace and mercy, which are brand new to you every single day, and to diligently guard your heart and keep it in a constant state of readiness to receive.

Review

For today's review, I want you to do a self-checkup on your progress of memorizing the first four *Resets*. If you have been reviewing them several times each day on this journey, you are probably doing great. Memorizing is easier for some; however, all of us can do it with enough repetition. Saying each *Reset* aloud to yourself and actually hearing your own voice will help a lot. Also, remember to be working on the Bible verses and memorizing them as well. The *Resets* and the verses are the reprogramming tools that will help you change your thinking. God will come alongside your efforts and transform you into a new person. I trust that the new input is already making adjustments in your core belief system and the way you look at life and how you react to your life's circumstances. Let the process continue to transform your attitudes, your feelings, your actions, and finally, the results in your life. Then you will be on your way to reclaiming the life that you should be living! This 28-day *reset* journey is just the beginning of learning to live life God's way. I congratulate you for your progress so far in this journey. In just a few more days, you will have seven *Resets* to continue using to grow in your new and revitalized relationship with God.

Reset #5

I diligently _____ ___ _____ to keep it _____ to _____ God's _____ grace and mercy, which are brand _____ to me every single_____.

This enables me to r____ peacefully in God's g_____ and to walk d_____ in His p_____.

"Guard your _____ above ____ _____, for it _____ the _____ of your life" Proverbs 4:23.

Today's Prayer

Dear God,

As I pray today, I pause now to remember the importance of guarding my heart so that it will always be receptive to receiving your daily provisions of grace and mercy. I do not want to miss your friendship today because I am too busy. Let Psalm 23 remind me again today of your desire to pursue me with your blessings, your overflowing goodness, and your unfailing love.

The Lord is my shepherd; I have all that I need.
He lets me rest in green meadows; he leads me beside peaceful streams.
He renews my strength. He guides me along right paths, bringing honor to his name.
Even when I walk through the darkest valley,
I will not be afraid, for you are close beside me.
Your rod and your staff protect and comfort me.
You prepare a feast for me in the presence of my enemies.
You honor me by anointing my head with oil.
My cup overflows with blessings.
Surely your goodness and unfailing love will pursue me all the days of my life, and I will live in the house of the Lord forever.
Amen.

Day 20

Real Rest Doesn't Come
in a Prescription Bottle

Let my soul be at rest again, for the
Lord has been good to me. **Psalm 116:7**

We started the second day of this *reset* journey considering how so many people today are experiencing such deep inner unrest about who they are and where they are going in life. You may have even recognized yourself in the middle of such a personal cycle of restlessness. You are like many other people and may have begun this 28-day journey with a desperate hope of recapturing a sense of inner peace and rest in your life.

If you ever just stop somewhere and watch people for a while, you can see restlessness written all over their faces and expressions. Even though the earth is still spinning on its axis at the same speed that it always has, it seems that life's frantic pace is breaking new speed records all the time. No matter what activities people are doing, many seem to be permanently stuck on the maximum speed setting in life's blender. Now I am not against using our time wisely and getting things done efficiently, but frantic is not my idea of a normal or healthy pace of living. Many people today multitask so constantly that they make the iconic Energizer Bunny look anemic! Did you see the video clip on TV where the mall patron was so preoccupied looking down at her smart phone that she walked, full-speed, right into the short wall that encircled the wishing-well fountain and tumbled into about two feet of water?

It is getting so epidemic that many people are even now having serious physical and mental medical symptoms related to the 24/7 overuse of all their latest technology gadgets. My wife even elbowed me a few weeks ago at church when she spotted a man in our row swiping his iPad screen, presumably following the sermon message on his Bible text application. Who knows if that is what he was really doing, but I still prefer to worship with my leather version of the Bible. I guess I would draw some attention too if I went biblically old-school one Sunday and showed up with my Scriptures printed on faded parchment in a neatly rolled up ancient-looking scroll. Can you imagine watching me try to find the pastor's announced biblical text by unrolling my Bible scroll and desperately searching for Habakkuk in the Old Testament?

Even though most of us sense the frantic pace that is all around us, and we think that we have our lives under control, it is still difficult not to get caught up in the tornado-like technology suction that is sweeping across the landscape of our modern culture. While pursuing our dreams, we feel like we have to have all of the latest stuff in order to fit in with everyone else. Could that be why so many families are way over their heads in debt today? It again goes back to one of the tactics of our spiritual enemy, to get our daily worldview focus off God and the blessings that He has for us. Rather, he lures us into constantly seeking after the things of this world, which are here today and outdated tomorrow. We keep chasing that elusive false happiness like a dog frantically chasing his tail around and around. Real and lasting happiness can only come from the inner contentment and peace of knowing God and relying on His goodness for our satisfaction. The second part of *Reset* #5 hits this ideal state of inner rest right on the head. Read it again and slowly focus on each word, allowing yourself to experience a fresh few moments of soul-relaxing quietness.

This enables me to rest peacefully in God's goodness and to walk daily in his presence.

As you learn and continue to repeat each *Reset* self-talk statement after this journey is completed, you will discover that certain *Reset* phrases will have extra meaning to you on different days. This phrase is one that I really like because it has such a soothing effect as I say it to myself. It relaxes my inner being like slow and deep breathing relaxes my physical body. As I remind myself to guard my heart and keep sin out, and knowing that I am continuously ready to receive fresh blessings for that day from God, I am enabled to experience a satisfying and peaceful rest throughout each day.

Where Does This Supernatural Rest Come From?

It all goes back again to the ultimate *reset* when God freed us from the weight of our sinfulness and the resulting separation from Him. Romans 5:1 say it perfectly: "Since we have been made right in God's sight by faith, we have peace with God because of what Jesus Christ our Lord has done for us." This supernatural, peaceful rest comes from God alone. You may have read some of the many popular magazine articles that describe all sorts of ways, including quiet meditation, physical exercise, and healthier eating, that we can utilize to find the road to inner peace. However, the God of the Bible is the only one who can sufficiently free us from the real source of our deep restlessness, our sins. With a cleansed heart, we are enabled to rest peacefully in God's goodness and to walk daily in His presence.

This Old Hymn Dating Back to 1889
Is Well Worth Remembering

I grew up playing hymns on the piano. Music has a way of getting into your head, and you never forget some of the words either. As I started writing this chapter, a particular hymn kept playing in my mind, so I went back and looked it up. It is entitled, "Wonderful Peace." Warren D. Cornell wrote the text, and W. George Cooper composed the tune back in 1889 at a Methodist camp meeting in West Bend, Wisconsin. This hymn has five verses and a chorus. The chorus is what has stuck in my mind for many years. I got out my old church hymnal and sat down to play it again. Wow! What a refreshing reminder of a great classic tune that churches from an earlier day used to sing as a testimony of a genuine inner heart experience. A heart set free is free indeed. In today's much busier and stressful generation, we would all do well to seek and pursue this kind of restful peace again. Here are those testimonial words from the second verse and chorus of that great old hymn.

What a treasure I have in this wonderful peace,
Buried deep in the heart of my soul;

So secure that no power can mine it away,
While the years of eternity roll.
Peace! peace! Wonderful peace,
Coming down from the Father above;
Sweep over my spirit forever I pray,
In fathomless billows of love.

There Are Two Kinds of Restlessness

This *reset* journey will help you with two kinds of restlessness. The first one we have already mentioned, and that is the restlessness of a soul separated by sin from God. The remedy for that condition comes when we receive and embrace Jesus as our personal Savior. Then we are forgiven and experience a deep, soul-satisfying resolution to our restlessness. The second kind of restlessness is a physical one. It comes from our chosen pace of life that we choose to live each day. This one creeps up on us today very easily. Our culture is driven by the concept that faster in almost everything is better! We can get so caught up in living at such a fast pace, that we are totally unaware of how fast we are going until we eventually crash and burn. The remedy for this restlessness is a much more personal one, and each one of us must find practical ways to adjust the pace of our lives. This usually involves complex decisions around our work, our families, and our leisure time. It is not always easy to do, but this can be something that you and God will have to work out together as you continue your new journey with Him.

Going back to *Reset #3*, this would be an excellent opportunity to talk to God about any areas or sources of restlessness in your life. Pray and ask Him for His help and guidance on how to adjust the pace of your life, so that you can learn to rest peacefully in the goodness that He pours out daily on you and your family. Managing our stresses in life can be a challenge for all people, Christians included. We are not immune from problems in this life. We face the same struggles, hardships, and tragedies as all people. However, we have a loving God who takes our hands, who gets under the table with us, and who walks with us through every hard place in life. Through Him, we can overcome and can be victorious in every circumstance of life. When we are weak in our own strength, God comes alongside us and reminds us of the very words that He declares about us in the Bible. Despite what everything else looks like around us, in those moments we can confidently believe by faith in the absolute authority and truth of God's viewpoint. 1 John 4:4 is a great reminder again of who wins the cosmic battle for the territory of your heart. "You belong to God . . . you have already won a victory . . . because the Spirit who lives in you is greater that the spirit who lives in the world." God wins the battle over Satan every time, but you must also do your part by diligently guarding your heart.

Recently, I was out with my wife for an evening of just browsing, or window-shopping as some would say. For quite some time, I had been looking for a ring that would be inspirational to wear. I had an idea of what I wanted, but I never could seem to discover the ring I was looking for. I was quite surprised one day when we walked into a little Christian gift shop near the beach where we now live. My eye caught a revolving rack that had all kinds of Christian trinkets, included some pewter rings. I almost moved on to the next rack, which was filled with music CDs, when my attention was pulled back to the rings. These rings were different from what I was looking for, but I saw a plain pewter ring with some engravings around it. When I lifted it off the hook to see what it said, I immediately knew it was perfect! I now wear that ring as a daily reminder because on it, it reads, "Greater is He that is in me." Each day, I know that God is my faithful source of victory and peace for both soul and physical restlessness.

It Comes From God—So Thank Him

This wonderful blessing comes from God. He is the source, and He enables you to experience it. The word *enable* means "to empower, to make possible, to allow, or to permit." God then enables you or makes it possible for you to rest peacefully.

Rest means "to pause, to take a breather, to be at ease, or to let up for a while." God enables you to be at ease because there is nothing that will come your way that you and He cannot handle together!

Peaceful means that you are "free from strife," or that you are "undisturbed or untroubled." So putting it all together, *God is the one who makes it possible for you to be at ease, because deep inside you are undisturbed and untroubled, no matter what is going on in the circumstances of your life.* Wow, that is something to pause right now and give God thanks for—His indescribable, wonderful, restful peace!

Review

Reset #____

__ _____ guard my _____ to keep it _____ to receive God's _____ grace and _____, which are brand ____ to ___ every _____ day.

This _____ me to r_____ p_____ in God's g_____ and to walk daily in His _____.

"Guard your _____ above ___ ____, for it _____ the course of your life" Proverbs ___:____.

Add these next two verses on the back of your fifth *Reset* card.

"Let my soul be at _____ again, for the Lord has been _____ to me" Psalm 116:7.

"I walk in the Lord's presence as I live here on the earth!" Psalm 116:9.

Today's Prayer

O God, my source of peace!

Thank you for making it possible for me to be at ease deep inside my being. You make it possible for me to experience real peace, the kind that causes me to be undisturbed and untroubled about the circumstances of my life. Even though I may go through hard places, you are greater and you provide overcoming victory each day of my life. So help me, O God, to do my part in diligently guarding my heart and keeping it ready. I desperately want to receive your grace and mercy each day. Let my soul be at rest again today. Help me to walk in your presence as I live here on the earth. This *reset* journey is blessing me, and it is transforming my life by helping me to change the way I think. It is true, God! You are so good, so ready to forgive, and so full of unfailing love for me when I ask for your help. Amen.

Day 21

A Trail Guide Who Knows the Trail Ahead

I walk in the Lord's presence as I live here on the earth! **Psalm 116:9**

The state of Colorado has some of the most beautiful places to take a young family exploring. When we lived in Colorado Springs, my wife and I would load up our minivan and take our sons on day drives up into the mountain trails in the Pikes Peak area. There were so many places to go and enjoy the day hiking, riding mountain bikes, eating picnic lunches, and, of course, taking pictures. Oh, I almost forgot Mollie! Remember, she was our black lab that we got as a rescue puppy. Those trips were wonderful for her with all the energy that she had stored up.

I can remember how all of us would need a little extra rest after a long, wonderful, exhausting day on the trails. The air is thinner in Colorado Springs because of its elevation of over six thousand feet. You get used to that altitude after living there for a while, but it was always challenging to be up on some of the area trails that approached Pikes Peak's elevation of fourteen thousand feet. According to one website, Pike's Peak is the most visited mountain in North America, and only second in the world to Japan's Mount Fuji. We had a great view of the Peak, even from our house in the city, which lies about ten miles to the east.

Several years ago, I was digging out boxes and sorting through twenty-plus years of old family pictures. I was putting together several collections of family pictures to hang on our walls to recapture and tell our family's history. A few pictures with breathtaking panoramic views from those days of hiking the mountain trails made the final cut to be included in the story-telling picture collections. One of my favorite pictures shows Jonathan and Jeremiah in their hiking boots, kneeling down, and posing on top of a huge boulder with their Colorado Rockies baseball hats on. Mollie, our black lab, is wedged between them with her slick black coat shining and her long wet tongue hanging out and panting. Behind this energetic trio is a spectacular Colorado backdrop, good enough for any promotional tourism brochure. Just looking at that picture again, I recall my silent prayer of thanks to God that day as I steadied the camera in my hand to freeze-frame that proud moment in time forever. I am so glad I took that picture. It reminds me now that I was their trail guide for that day, but God was the greater trail guide for me as their dad, trying to do my best to nurture them during those critical formative years.

As we conclude our look today at *Reset* #5, our focus will be on the last phrase. In addition to resting peacefully in God's goodness, you are also enabled "to walk daily in His presence." At the beginning of this journey, we laid out the sequence of how changing the way you think transforms you into a new person. This is why you are memorizing each *Reset* statement and using them daily to give yourself a good, healthy dose of self-talk. This biblically based self-talk is much more positive and encouraging than perhaps what you used to say to yourself. You are now evicting and replacing old, self-defeating talk with powerful words and life-changing phrases based on the authority and reliability of God's Word.

In just three weeks, your new input is literally transforming your core beliefs about God, about yourself, and about the possibility of you reclaiming the life you should be living. Along with that, your attitudes and feelings about your life in general, where you have been, where you are now, and where you are going in the future, are experiencing a brand-new perspective. It is as if you have had corrective eye surgery. Not only can you see the big picture of your life more clearly, but now you see it as God wants you to see it. With these new perspectives and your daily reviews of our self-talk *Resets* for this journey, you should be noticing some growing tendencies to act or behave differently than you used to. In short, God is transforming your life little by little, allowing you to become more like the person He created you to be.

An Old Testament Example of Walking with God in a Messed Up World

The story of Noah in the Old Testament book of Genesis is a good illustration of how possible it is to live a life pleasing to God, even in the midst of a corrupt and immoral culture. Noah, it seems, was the only one who worshiped God. It was a wicked generation that he lived in, and Noah endured much ridicule for his worldview and faith in God. His obedience to build the Ark to God's specific directions was not only time consuming, but made him the prime material for jokes throughout the region. Can you imagine the heyday that modern late-night talk show hosts would have had with material like that? Noah and his crazy ark-building antics in the midst of drought-like conditions would have been the proverbial gift that just kept giving.

The lesson I take from Noah's story is that if we gain God's favor by doing what is right, even in the midst of everyone else doing what is wrong, God will find us and walk faithfully with us. If you get the chance, go pick up Noah's story in Genesis 6, and read the rest of the story. God never abandoned and never forgot Noah, who was apparently the only righteous man in all the earth at the time. Noah kept believing God and persisted admirably through those tough times. God was faithful to bless his obedience and saved his whole family from the epic flood that destroyed the world. If God would walk daily with Noah and be his guide in life because of his faithful obedience, then you and I should not settle for anything less. I think it is time to choose God as our trail guide for life's entire journey.

Who Do You Want on the Journey with You?

Our third supporting verse for this *Reset* is so simple. "I walk in the Lord's presence as I live here on the earth!" (Psalm 116:9). This self-talk verse right out of Scripture is in the present tense. It does not declare that I used to walk with God or that I sometimes walk with God or that I will one day walk with God. No, it emphatically declares that I am now walking, today, in God's presence and will continue to walk in His presence.

Most of the mountain trails that we used to hike in Colorado were park trails, opened to the public and complete with adequate signs to mark the right trails to stay on and to follow. The signs would usually give you some helpful information, such as how long the trail was and how difficult the terrain was for hiking. However, it was always smart to carry a real trail guide or map to keep from accidently getting lost or making a wrong turn down a dangerous trail. You did not want to stray into areas that would be too treacherous to safely navigate! Because I wasn't a lifelong resident, it was even more helpful if a seasoned hiker of those trails could be our guide for the day and ensure a fun, but safe day of hiking. I always felt much better having someone like that who had traveled those trails many times before and knew everything about them that I did not know. A personal guide could take us down an unknown path to give us a breathtaking view that I would never have known about. On the other hand, he could be there to warn us of impending dangerous and slippery portions of the trail just ahead.

God promises to be that kind of trail guide for us on our daily journey through this life. Most of us have not fully realized the close, intimate walk that is possible with God. Could it be that there are so few role models, just like in Noah's day? Perhaps it just seems too unlikely and improbable that anyone could actually walk in the presence of God. Yet that is the simple claim of Scripture. It clearly implies that one can walk in the presence of the Lord as he or she lives here on the earth! Now we all know the good feeling that comes when we take a nice refreshing walk with a good friend, just talking and sharing what is on our hearts and minds. How good would it be if we would start having that same kind of spiritual walk with God on a daily basis? Apparently, that is the literal bold assumption of Scripture. In Psalm 116:9, the word *walk* implies a personal and steady travel on foot, taking one routine step at a time in order to proceed on our journey through life, one day at a time. "In the Lord's presence" is a phrase that refers to being in His close company or proximity, or better yet, intimately being in His immediate circle. It is the opposite idea of being extremely detached and distant.

Does God Really Get Specific and Show Me the Way to Go?

Another way we often ask this question is, *How can I know the will of God for my life?* Many people have tried to share their thoughts on this difficult subject. I have read many books on how to pray for God's wisdom or how to abstain from food and fast for a season to sharpen my spiritual senses to better discern God's will. There are speakers who claim certain techniques of meditation will provide avenues to understanding God's will. While there is truth in all these and other attempts, let me share a simple answer that I have been focusing on from an excellent daily devotional book by Henry T. Blackaby and Richard Blackaby, called *Experiencing God Day-By-Day*. This is what they say:

> If you are walking daily with the Lord, you will not have to find God's will—you will already be in it. If you are walking with Him in obedience day by day, you will always be in the will of God. The Holy Spirit's role is to guide you step by step to do God's will. Walking closely with God each day guarantees that you will be exactly where He wants you to be.[1]

It is probably safe for me to say that most of us have not yet reached that level of intimate walking with God. Nevertheless, it should be our priority and earnest goal to have that kind of daily walk with God. Something that wonderful should be our constant desire. Can you imagine the unbroken relationship that Adam and Even must have experienced with God in the garden of Eden before they sinned and disobeyed God? It is only with sin not present in our hearts that we can move closer to our desired intimate walk with God. That is why our fifth *Reset* statement says that we will diligently guard our hearts to keep sin out and to keep our hearts ready to walk daily in the presence of God.

God Knows the Way Ahead of You Right Now!

If there is anything I know about God, it is that He is completely sovereign. He knows my name. He knows my past. He knows my present. He knows my future. He knows it all when it comes to my daily journey on this earth. No one else knows all of that. There is no credible source, other than God, that can tell me how to best navigate my way in this life. Wherever you are today in your life's journey, you must believe that it is possible to walk in the Lord's presence as you live out your days here on the earth. God knows every day that you have left to live on this earth. He knows every trail that you will have to walk on. Some of life's trails will have obvious signs to mark your way. Others will provide no direction, and some may prove to be treacherous. Without God's presence to guide you, you will find it extremely hard on many days to discern which way is the best way for you to go.

Do not be like many clueless people who seem to follow the advice, "When you come to a fork in the road, take it!" Decide to start now and practice walking daily in God's presence and discover that as you do that more and more, you are perhaps already in God's will for your life. I think that was Noah's secret to living in such a wicked generation. He had a clean heart, he walked daily in the presence of God, and he found favor in God's eyes.

Even though you may not know too many people today who have this kind of close walk with God, you could be the first one to do it in your family or in your neighborhood. Start guarding your heart because it does determine the course of your life. Keep it ready to receive God's overflowing grace and mercy each day. With a clean heart and mind, you will then be able to rest peacefully in God's goodness and to walk daily in His close proximity.

Review

Today we finished up with *Reset #5*. Tomorrow we will introduce *Reset #6*, and soon after that we will be sharing *Reset #7*, which will give you a great self-talk to begin and end each day. For your review today, there are no blanks to fill in. However, I do want you to pull out your five *Reset* cards and review them, along with the verses until you are getting them down in your memory word-for-word. It may be tempting to take this review time lightly or not do it at all. Even if you just repeat each *Reset* five times a day, it will help you retain them even after you finish the 28-day journey. Plus, the more you say them aloud to yourself with sincere conviction, the more you are reprogramming and changing the way you think. So get those cards out and enjoy the progress you have made so far.

Today's Prayer

Dear God,

I want to thank you again for bending down to personally hear and answer me when I pray and ask for your help and guidance. When I started this 28-day journey, personally walking with you was not something I had really ever done well, if at all. In fact, I was like most people and felt good if I just went to church. I had never really thought about the huge difference between knowing about God and walking with God. I am still captivated with the initial thought that I am on your mind again today and that I really do matter to you. I know that I am changing, because I find that you are on my mind more too. Help me in the daily battle to guard my heart, and may I learn to rest peacefully in your goodness. Amen.

RESET #6

Day 22

What Will You Decide to Do Next?

Yesterday we concluded *Reset* #5, which focuses on the importance of diligently guarding your heart. This will always be one of your greatest challenges, and you will never be completely successful at it 100 percent of the time. However, if you will utilize that self-talk *Reset* every day and say it to yourself, especially during the strategic moments of negative thought attacks or temptations to do wrong, then you will be much more effective in keeping your heart ready to receive God's daily provision of overflowing grace and mercy. The more you are successful in guarding your heart, the more you will sense that you are walking in the presence of God throughout your day.

Today, we introduce *Reset* #6 to you by sharing a quote from Shad Helmstetter, the author of an in-depth book on the subject of self-talk.

What you decide to do next will determine what you do next.[1]

You might have to reread that statement a few times to realize the simple, but powerful truth contained in it. It is so obvious that after I first read it many years ago, I have allowed it to sit prominently on my mind's memory shelf, frequently reminding me of how important my moment-by-moment daily decisions in life are. Most of the time, the big decisions and events in life stick out in retrospect much more than the smaller daily decisions. We tend to remember those big events or decisions more because they had a major impact on the direction of our lives. Sometimes the outcome of a decision was good and other times it was not so good. For example, maybe you made a decision in the past about which college to attend or which job to take. Looking back, that may or may not have been the best choice. Maybe a decision was about whether to marry a particular person. Maybe it was about whether to work through a rough place in your marriage or jump ship and pull the plug. Perhaps someone else made a critical decision without your input that tragically altered the direction or circumstances of your life.

These and many other big decisions in life obviously affect the direction and course of our lives. However, the hour-by-hour daily decisions are equally huge because they are the ones that ultimately shape our character and influence our lives at the very cores of our being. With that in mind, how we make the many daily routine choices is very important. If Helmstetter's statement is true, "what you decide to do next will determine what you do next," then it would be helpful to have some navigational help in making our decisions and mapping out our courses on the road of life.

God's Way Is Always Best!

During my days as a children's pastor, I enjoyed working with my ministry teams to develop a focus on what our purpose would be in working with children. We clarified and stated specially that our vision was to "help families get their kids on God's team and become real winners in life." In order to formulate a phrase that children of all ages could easily learn, we adopted this motto: "God's way is always best!"

We also determined that we would constantly work that phrase into our weekly lessons as we nurtured the children from birth through elementary school age in our church. I would tell kids, "Someday you are going to be a little older and facing some really tough choices. Some of your friends may start doing some things that are not right and ask you to join them. On the other hand, you may have to make some important decisions about how you will live your lives. When that day comes, if you remember only one thing that we are trying to teach you, remember this: God's way is always best! Then make your choices by determining what God's way is concerning the decision that you must make. If you do not know the answer right away, then go to the Bible or to a trusted friend and find out first what God's way is before you make your decision. If you do that and always follow Him, you will know that you have made the best decision. God will honor you for that, and He will lead you in the way that you should go."

Now, let us combine the thought behind that simple motto with the earlier quote. It then becomes clear that when we decide what we will do next (keeping in mind that God's way is always best), then that choice will determine that our next action will be pleasing to God.

Suppose you were the captain of a ship, and you were on a long journey across the seas. You would chart your course and then follow your route carefully. In order to stay on the proper course, you would have to make many hourly navigational adjustments or decisions depending on the changing variables of the sea and the weather conditions. As you continue today on this 28-day *reset* journey, here is a new short self-talk statement that will consistently help you make the best choices in life when you are considering what to do next. Just make sure that you are clearly determining what God's way is. Write this *Reset* out on your sixth index card.

Reset #6

I will navigate life's journey today and make my daily choices knowing that God's way is always best.

Now write this supportive Bible verse on the back of your card.

"I am the Lord your God, who teaches you what is good for you and leads you along the paths you should follow" (Isaiah 48:17).

Let's Take a Closer Look

The last part of our newest *Reset* states that we know God's way is always best for us. That is a bold thing to say, and you must believe deep in your heart that it is true. So how can we be so sure that God's way is always best? Again, if we believe that God is our authoritative and reliable source of truth, what does His Word say about this? For starters, our supportive verse, Isaiah 48:17, is clear and quotes God himself. "I am the Lord your God, who teaches you what is good for you and leads you along the paths you should follow." Wow! If God is going to teach and guide me on a daily basis, then I can feel good about that being the best of all possible ways for me to make my decisions in life.

DAVID STEVENS

Another classic verse about God's guidance in our lives is Jeremiah 29:11-13: "For I know the plans I have for you," says the Lord. "They are plans for good and not for disaster, to give you a future and a hope. In those days when you pray, I will listen. If you look for me wholeheartedly, you will find me." In these verses, we strongly sense that God has a specific plan or a purpose for our lives. Even though we might not always know all the details of His plan, we can know with absolute certainty that His plans are good for us.

Furthermore, we also know from Romans 8:28 that "God causes everything to work together for the good of those who love God." That includes the good and the bad circumstances or events in our lives. Therefore, during those times in your life when everything is messed up and falling apart, there is still hope for a better day and a better outcome. Even when your vision of the journey ahead is limited, like driving your car on a dark, damp, foggy night on a narrow and curvy two-lane country road, you can at least know that it is still best to move forward in faith and to follow God's guiding hand.

Let take a closer look at several key words in our newest *Reset* statement. When we think of the word *know*, it brings up the connotation of confidence and of certainty. When we know something with certainty, we are positive that it is rock solid and true.

That reminds me of a funny story about a boy whose father asked him one evening how he had done on an important test that day at school. The boy quickly responded, "I didn't do very well, Dad. In fact, I think I probably failed the test." To that comment, the Dad tried to encourage him and responded, "Well, don't be so negative. Could you not be more positive than that?" The boy took his cue and quickly revised his statement. "Okay Dad, I'm positive that I failed the test!"

So now that we know or can be confidently certain that God's way is always best, what does the word *always* imply? Simply, it means every single time, on every occasion, and without exception. Furthermore, the word *best* means most desirable, superior, unrivaled, finest, or the most excellent.

So when you now say *Reset* #6 to yourself and repeat the phrase, "God's way is always best," you are literally saying that *every single time and on every occasion, God's way is without exception the most desirable, superior, unrivaled, finest, and most excellent way to go.*

162

Review

As we enter our last week of this 28-day journey, you know the importance of doing your daily review. Keep working on all of the previous *Reset* self-talk statements and verses. Today, add *Reset #6* and Isaiah 48:17 to what you are learning and memorizing.

Focus your thoughts throughout today on the phrase that we just highlighted, *God's way is always best!* On a scale of one to ten, how would you rate your current belief that God's way is always best?

Try to fill in the blanks.

Reset #6

I will n_____ life's j_____ today and make my daily c_____ knowing that God's _____ is _____ _____.

"I am the Lord your _____, who teaches you what is g_____ for you and l_____ you along the paths you should f_____" Isaiah 48:17.

Today's Prayer

Dear God,

This *reset* journey has opened my eyes to make me aware of your great love for me and how much you want to help me live my life and enjoy a close, daily relationship with you. Today, you have reminded me of a clear truth that I want to believe with all my heart. As I navigate through life and as I make my daily choices, I truly want to know and believe with absolute certainty that your way is always best for my life. On every single occasion in my life and without exception, your way will be the most desirable and unrivaled option for me. Help me to discern each day and in each situation what your way is for me. Thank you for being that kind of intimate and personal God to me, and for offering to guide me each day and working all things together for good in my life. Amen.

Day 23

Beware of the Autopilot Setting

Imagine yourself settling down into window Seat A on Row 8 at 6:42 a.m., getting ready for your scheduled 6:55 a.m. takeoff. You are taking a transcontinental flight from New York to Los Angeles for a much-needed week of relaxation and sightseeing. Flight attendants' eyes are busy scanning the length of the narrow aisle, making sure that everyone is in his or her seat properly and that the overhead bins are securely closed. The required emergency instructions are completed, and just as the flight attendants take their seats, you suddenly feel the initial thrust of the powerful engines throttling up to begin their task of rapidly propelling the airplane down the runway. Out of habit, you take a deep breath and slowly exhale to relax yourself, knowing that soon you will be airborne and that you will be able to settle back and begin reading a brand-new novel on your Kindle.

All is well as you look out the window over your left shoulder at an emerging, beautiful sunrise, accentuated by a brilliant yellow cotton ball-like cloud formation suspended out on the distant eastern horizon. Finally, after a hectic morning commute that almost made you late, a dreadfully slow check-in to drop off your luggage and to obtain your boarding pass, and then finally inching through the long security lines, you are now thankful and feeling a little lucky that your seat has a perfect view of such a glorious sight. Your only hope now is that the pilot will not have to bank the plane too quickly once you are airborne. The view of this sunrise from above the early morning haze of the city should be fantastic!

After a few thankful minutes of absorbing more of the inspirational sunrise, the plane does start to bank to the right slowly, turning its nose toward its westward destination as it continues its climb to cruising altitude. The awaited announcement comes on that it is now safe to operate your electronic devices, so you reach down to retrieve your Kindle and start reading your much-anticipated new novel.

As you release the power button and the book's cover page emerges on your Kindle's screen, an automated but clear, mechanical-sounding, monotone male voice begins to speak through the speakers of the plane's cabin.

"Good morning! We welcome you this morning for this exciting, new day in aviation history. Today, you are the first passengers aboard the historic inaugural Flight 256, nonstop from New York to Los Angeles. We count it a privilege to have you with us today, and our flight attendants will soon be handing you a commemorative pin as a keepsake for this special occasion. In fact, the president of the United States will be speaking at a brief ceremony to honor this flight on the tarmac upon our arrival in Los Angeles.

"Today's flight is the very first commercial passenger flight to be piloted by computer only. There are no pilots or copilots onboard this flight in the cockpit area. Yes, that is right! You have just experienced the first computerized, autopilot take-off ever, and soon we will reach our cruising altitude. Our computerized landing has already been safely programmed into the system, and we should be arriving in Los Angeles slightly ahead of schedule. The technology for this historic aviation feat has been developed and tested over many years. All flight systems have been thoroughly checked, so we invite you to sit back, relax, and enjoy the flight, because nothing possible could go wrong . . . go wrong . . . go wrong . . . go wrong . . . go wrong . . ."

Suddenly, your novel can wait!

You and I Have Access to the Most Qualified and Reliable Pilot

If we are not careful, we can easily find ourselves navigating through life relying on ourselves or on an autopilot setting to guide us. Without much thought, we will then find ourselves going along with the flow of an ungodly culture and not really paying much attention to how many of our basic daily choices might be in direct conflict with God's way.

Let us look again today at our Bible verse from Isaiah 48:17: "I am the Lord your God, who teaches you what is good for you and leads you along the paths you should follow." If we truly believe that God will lead us to make daily choices that are the best ones for our lives, then we should never rely on ourselves or on an autopilot setting. In fact, you and I must specifically make sure that we invite and allow God to be the primary pilot of our lives. If God is not the one we rely on to pilot our lives, then either we will take the controls ourselves or simply engage the autopilot setting and blindly hope for the best. If we do choose to engage the autopilot, then there is a good chance that the enemy of our souls will try to jump in and override the autopilot setting, accomplishing his own dual purposes of steering you way off the right course and effectively keeping you separated from God. He will deceptively and skillfully use that as a daily strategy and tactic to steal, kill, and destroy God's plan for your life.

I like the fact that Isaiah 48:17 is directly quoting God himself. When God says something firsthand, we receive an emphatic promise, delivered in clear, simple terms of not only who the promise is from, but also what He will do, and what the destination or outcome will be. As I read the verse word-for-word, I visualize first that God is standing before me, emphasizing my personal relationship with Him. He then implies the reliability of His faithful character, and tells me that He will teach me or tutor me one-on-one, specifically promising to point out what is good for me, and assuring me that He will only lead me along the right paths that I should be following.

With that kind of promise, the decision should be a no-brainer. But Satan is the master deceiver, and just like he did with Adam and Eve in the garden of Eden, Satan's same strategy is to try to convince you that God only wants to withhold all the really good stuff in life from you. If Satan can get you to believe that same lie all over again, then you will be doomed to the same destructive consequences of Adam and Eve's rebellious choice.

Let it be perfectly clear here: God is the only one that you and I should even consider turning the control of our lives over to. Even though we might not often be able to see far down the road ahead of us, knowing that God is guiding us and that His way is always best, we can fearlessly trust Him for each step and for each stage of our journey. Will you make that choice today to allow God to be the daily pilot and right-every-time guide for your life? Once you make that decision, then it will come down to trusting God each day and obeying His directions as He gives them. It reminds me again of another hymn that I used to play on the piano with these familiar words.

When we walk with the Lord, In the light of His Word,
What a glory He sheds on our way!
While we do His good will, He abides with us still,
And with all who will trust and obey.
Trust and obey, For there's no other way,
To be happy in Jesus, But to trust and obey.

Life's Journey Is Still One Day at a Time

The hardest thing for most people who want to follow God daily is learning to be patient. That probably explains why patience comes in at number four on the Apostle Paul's list of nine fruits of the Spirit found in Galatians 5, only behind love, joy, and peace. Patience does not come to most of us by nature, especially in our fast-paced society. Be honest! When was the last time you sought out the longest line at Walmart to make your purchase?

We are always looking for the shortcuts in life. Parents today are even depriving their young children of what used to be considered a slower-paced, normal childhood by pushing them into too many activities before they are even out of kindergarten. In America, we can even trace many of our personal weight control issues to our addictions to a fast-food lifestyle. To summarize, as adults, we often get impatient and wish that God would just give us the complete road map to our whole lives and futures all at once. In our instant gratification, high-tech world, where even over-night postal delivery seems like the slow days of the pony express, our expectations are so unrealistic that we jokingly pray, "Lord, please give me more patience right now!" I even remember a one-frame cartoon where the caption was, "The main problem with life is that it is so daily." Somehow, we must recover some balance in our schedules and slow down enough to enjoy life and spend some daily time with God on our journey. Yes, life is still "so daily," as the cartoon said, and it is still broken up into consistent twenty-four-hour periods. When the sun comes up each morning, we have just one portion of the journey allotted for us to navigate and travel that day. When there are so many options and ungodly paths to choose from, we would be wise to accept God's daily offer to teach us what way is good for us and then to follow Him as He leads us along the right path for our journey.

Why not decide today to let God take over the responsibilities of guiding you and safely helping you navigate each day's portion of your life's journey. Beware of the autopilot setting. If you settle for that, you will soon wake up and realize that your life is not in control . . . not in control . . . not in control . . . not in control.

Review

Do you remember early in our journey when I shared my story about the greeting card that got me thinking about writing *The Reset?* It had on the front, "Thinking Of You." Then on the inside, it said, "Just thought I would say hello, for you were on my mind." As we come down to the last few days of our journey together, I am already starting to think about the day when you read the last page and you close this book.

I used to have the same feelings years ago when my family of four used to meet up with members of my family and about fifteen to twenty of our close aunts, uncles, and cousins at the beach each year in June. We all shared a large, five bedroom, rented beach house with a full screened-in front porch, lined with wooden rocking chairs, for a week. Each year on Thursday of that week, I would start regretting the thought that Saturday was coming and that we would all be soon saying our good-byes, giving our hugs, and departing in different directions to go back to our homes in various states. Life would then resume its previous, predictable routines, and we would again start counting the months until next year's family beach gathering.

In a way, I feel that way now about these last few days of my journey with you. However, I do not want your *reset* journey to end on Day 28 and then you simply go back to resuming your previous predictable routine, especially your old way of thinking about God and your relationship, or lack of one, with Him.

That is why I have given you these *Resets* to memorize word-for-word. My hope is that your life is beginning to experience a genuine transformation as you are allowing God to change the way you think. But this 28-day journey can only help you get started. After you close the book, I want you to let each of the seven *Resets* continue to transform your life. You do not have to go back to your previous ways of thinking. You have already evicted some of your old, negative, and self-defeating thoughts and have replaced them with biblically-based, positive self-talk statements. You also know now how God really feels about you. You really do matter to Him! He wants to have a daily relationship with you, and He will answer your prayers. If you let Him, when you finally close this book, He will also gladly guide your life from that day forward and always show you the way that you should go.

I really care about you too! Even though I might not know you personally, through the writing of this book, I have pictured myself sharing these *Resets* with all kinds of people like you, who would like to reclaim the lives that they should be living. I used to share simple Bible truths with children gathered around me each week, always teaching them "God's way is always best!" Through this book journey, I hope to reach many more people and help restore their intimate relationships and daily walks with God.

If you will continue to review your *Resets* each day and continue doing so after you put this book down, then I will feel that we have become like friends, in that we are all reclaiming and enjoying the same kind of life that God wants all of us to share with him!

I will _____ _____ _____ today and make my _____
_____ knowing that God's _____ ___ _____ _____.

"I am the Lord your God, who _____ you what is good for you and _____ you along the paths you should _____" Isaiah 48:17.

Today's Prayer

Dear heavenly Father,

Thank you for the reality of a true friendship with you. First, you have spoken to me on this journey and made me aware of your deep desire to befriend me through the work of your son, Jesus, on the cross. He died and rose again to show me the way back to you and to tear down the wall that sin created as a barrier between us.

Secondly, I sense that I have met new friends through the reading of this book, which has put us on a shared journey for 28 days! The Bible teaches that where two or three get together in your name, you are there in spirit with them. I guess that same principle can somewhat apply when two or three share a 28-day *reset* book journey together. Your presence, God, brings our hearts and minds together, and we share the real joy and strength of seeking you on the same journey. Amen.

Day 24

Make Sure You Are Connected to the Original GPS

Last year, my wife and I went on a day trip with our friends and neighbors, the Savidges, to Charleston, South Carolina. We planned it to be a day of fun, sightseeing, and a nice lunch somewhere. The drive from Myrtle Beach to Charleston is maybe two hours down Highway 17, passing through Pawley's Island and Georgetown on the way. The weather was beautiful, and we had a great time together with our friends, who split up their year by living seven months in South Carolina and five months in New York.

The Savidges insisted on taking their car, a Toyota Prius. Even though we knew where we were going, they decided to turn on their Garmin GPS. For some reason, we got to talking about the default voice of the lady giving us our directions on the Garmin. We all decided that she was a little too loud when she kept rudely interrupting our conversation, so I was delegated the task of turning her down. That action quickly turned into too much fun for me. I proceeded to lead four grown adults into listening to every optional voice that we could choose from if we decided to override the default voice of our rude lady friend. It was hilarious listening to all the different voices with various accents, dialects, and even a variety of foreign languages. We eventually went back to the original default female voice, but I did turn her down to a lower volume. From that time on, we affectionately called her Gertrude. As you might guess, we had a great time with our friends on our day trip to Charleston!

Anyone who has a GPS device in his or her vehicle knows that they are great for helping us navigate a journey or trip, starting from one place and ending at our chosen destination. They give us continuous, invaluable information all along the way, such as how far to drive until the next turn or road change, how far the journey is in miles or kilometers, and the estimated time of arrival. These GPS systems have become so common that younger drivers see no need for the traditional Rand McNally road map, which has been standard equipment in the trunk of many cars for years.

If you own a GPS system, you know that the most annoying word in the GPS vocabulary is "recalculating!" Whenever you choose to deviate at all from your GPS's preferred directions, you will hear that word within seconds, followed by an alternative route to help you reach your destination. Sometimes, I want to go into a large parking lot, drive around in circles and see how much patience Gertrude has with me, or if she will just finally lose it. GPS technology has so rapidly expanded and been so accepted that it is now hard to imagine getting around in life without our GPS devices and smart phone apps to help us.

This *Reset* Is All about the Original and Most Reliable GPS!

When you receive and embrace Jesus as your personal Savior, you are spiritually connected to God the Father, Jesus the Son, and the Holy Spirit. One of your primary benefits in that triune relationship is the ability to receive God's daily guidance for living. In our sixth *Reset*, which we will conclude today, you are declaring to yourself your intent to use and rely on the original and most reliable GPS ever. That GPS would be Jesus, who guides you through the Holy Spirit. Yes, He will lead and guide you throughout each day's journey, if you will let Him. He is the original and most reliable GPS, our Great Personal Savior!

It All Comes Down to Your Choice of Where You Place Your Trust

Here are the words penned by Joseph Gilmore, later put to music as a hymn by William B. Bradbury and published in 1864, long before we had GPS devices in our cars.

He leadeth me! O blessed thought!
O words with heavenly comfort fraught!
Whate'er I do, where'er I be, Still 'tis God's hand that
leadeth me!
He leadeth me, He leadeth me, By His own hand He
leadeth me:
His faithful follower I would be, For by His hand He
leadeth me.

This hymn gives us the picture of God personally leading us by hand, and that becomes a blessed thought to the individual who navigates through life wholeheartedly trusting in God's daily guidance. God is all-knowing and all-powerful. Nothing escapes His eye as He watches over us. He causes all things to work together ultimately for good in our lives. Sometimes we will never know why God does what He does and why He allows certain things to happen in our lives. However, when we place our complete trust in Him and in His goodness, then we can make our daily choices, knowing with confidence that His way is always best!

A well-known verse to many people is Proverbs 3:5-6. "Trust in the Lord with all your heart; do not depend on your own understanding. Seek his will in all you do and he will show you which path to take."

It can be easy to read and even memorize this verse and still not live by it. Why? It is human nature to want to do things our way and not God's way. Furthermore, to trust God with part of our hearts or only when it is convenient, seems to be much easier for most people than to completely trust Him with our whole hearts all the time.

Therefore, it comes down to a determined, willful choice and selection of a navigational GPS for your personal life. Our sixth *Reset* is a daily, present-tense decision for you to navigate each day's journey and to make your hour-by-hour choices, knowing with confident certainty in your heart that God's way is always best. This is key to whether you will either win or lose the many strategic battles in your life. Make the decision today to connect with the original and most reliable GPS. That would be Jesus, your Great Personal Savior!

It will be helpful for you to use this sixth *Reset* often in your life. Again, that is why you need to memorize each of the seven *Reset* statements and continue utilizing them after our 28-day book journey is complete. Do you remember in the introductory chapter when we imagined a day-ending highlight video showing your "shining moments" for the day? The more you learn to make your daily choices with your Great Personal Savior (GPS) guiding you, the more you will enjoy reviewing that day-ending highlight video in your mind. You will wrap up your day often thanking God for His help and guidance. Of course, there will be days when you make your mistakes, but you will humbly pray and ask God to forgive you and help you make better choices tomorrow. Never forget our first *Reset*, which says that you are on still on God's mind, even if you just messed up.

As a final thought, remember that you cannot make your best daily decisions in life by simply relying on how you feel about something. Feelings can often be deceptive, and Satan will try his best to distort the truth by trying to get you to focus on your feelings. The truth is that *God's way is always best,* and that should guide your daily choices in life. That truth, or input, now forms your core beliefs, which determines your attitudes. Your attitudes then affect your feelings, which play out in your daily actions, which bring about the results that are best in your life.

INPUT—CORE BELIEFS—ATTITUDES— FEELINGS—ACTIONS—RESULTS

Review (Fill in the blanks and either quote or review the verses)

Reset #1

I am on God's _____ again today.
  (even if I just _____ up)

I really do _____ to God and He is always thinking
_____ _____ about me.

Today, I will let God be ___ ____ _____ too.

Romans 12:2
Psalm 139:17

Reset #2

I believe that God _____, that his _____ is true, and that real joy and strength are my _____ for _____ him.

Hebrews 11:6
Nehemiah 8:10

Reset #3

I now visualize God _____ down to personally _____ and _____ me when I _____ and _____ for his _____ and _____.

Psalm 86:1
Psalm 86:5

Reset #4

I _____ and _____Jesus as my personal Savior, and I now enjoy my _____ of being _____ _____ with God _____.

I am a _____ of God based on _____ and _____.

Psalm 116:4
Romans 10:13
Romans 10:9-10

Reset #5

I diligently _____ my _____ to keep it ready to _____ God's overflowing _____ and _____, which are brand _____ to me every single day.

This enables me to rest _____ in God's _____ and to walk _____ in his _____.

Proverbs 4:23
Psalm 116:7
Psalm 116:9

Reset #6

I will _____ life's _____ today and make my _____
_____ knowing that God's _____ is always _____.

Isaiah 48:17

Today's Prayer

Dear God,

So many times, I have tried to navigate my own journey and calculate my own direction in life without considering that your way is always best. Starting today, I want to let Jesus be my Great Personal Savior, my GPS. Like the hymn writer, I want to end each day being able to say: "He leadeth me! O blessed thought . . . His faithful follower I will be, for by His hand He leadeth me!" I believe that will further enable me to rest peacefully in your goodness and to walk daily in your presence. Thank you again, O God, for coming close to me during this *reset* journey and helping me reclaim the life that I am now learning to live in a right relationship with you. Amen.

RESET #7

Day 25

The Smartest Thing You Can Ever Do to Begin and End Each Day!

I am trusting in you, O Lord, saying, "You are my God!"
My future is in your hands. **Psalm 31:14-15**

After someone that you are close to betrays your trust, it is extremely difficult to trust other people again. I can think back to several times in my life when people who I thought I could trust the most decided to disregard their commitments to our relationships and behaved in a way that caused me tremendous hurt and pain. In fact, the encouragement card that I received from my Aunt Theresa that I mentioned on Day 3 came after my most devastating betrayal of trust when I was much younger. Those were difficult days for me, but God taught me a lot about His faithfulness, and He eventually used that betrayal to make me a much stronger person. Earlier, I also referred to the song by Andrae Crouch called, "Through It All." I can still remember how that song helped me to lean hard on God and to trust Him to get me through those days of struggling with disillusionment. One of my favorite lines in the song reminded me "to depend upon His Word," and from that encouragement, I started memorizing Bible verses that brought healing and restoration to my broken heart.

I am sure that you have also been the victim of many disappointments and betrayals in your life. None of us are immune from such trials, and you better get used to the idea that difficult days will find their way into your datebook. Most of us have learned to deal with normal, everyday disappointments fairly well. It is just those times when people jerk everything out from under us that it hurts so much. When we invest a special part of our life in a relationship with another person and then that person betrays us without ever considering reconciliation, it becomes easy not to trust another person ever again.

Today, we are introducing our last *Reset* statement, which deals directly with this issue of trust. Let me state something clearly here. *Trusting God is one of the most liberating and healing things that you will ever learn to do.* Somewhere in your past, another family member or friend may have betrayed your trust when you were a child. Perhaps you had a marriage dissolved by a breach of trust. Maybe you lost a job because of the mishandling of a trust-related issue. I could go on and give more possible examples of trust-related disappointments in life that might still be holding you back from ever trusting anyone again, especially God. Right now, can you specifically think of some event or some person in your past that might still be keeping you from trusting God? It might be a little painful to dig it up and remember it right now, and most likely, it would be a whole lot easier to keep it buried. However, God completely understands your hurt, and He would like to bring healing to that specific disappointment in your life. In doing just that, God also has a deep desire to renew His relationship with you and to enable you to have your trust in Him completely restored again.

That is where our seventh and final *Reset* is going to help you. The purpose of this 28-day *reset* journey has been to help you reclaim the life you should be living in a relationship with God. Trust is something that God wants to restore in your life, and He can definitely do it. It is also something that you will have to nurture on your own as well. If you will let this *Reset* help you renew and strengthen your trust in God, I believe that you will discover what I have personally learned over many years. *A real, good, honest gauge of your relationship with God is the level of your day-to-day total trust in Him.*

On your seventh index card, write down the first phrase of this last *Reset* statement (tomorrow we will give you the last phrase).

> I begin and end each day trusting God
> wholeheartedly with His plans for my future.

That is it! Simple, but so necessary to completing the process of reclaiming the life you should be living. Even though you may have deep wounds from having your trust betrayed by others in your past, do not let your trust in God suffer another day because of what they did. Your relationship with God has probably already improved on this journey, so continue the progress by saying this *Reset* aloud to yourself until it becomes a reality for you.

The supportive verse for this was quoted at the beginning of this chapter. Here it is again. Write this Bible verse on the top half of the back of your seventh index card.

"I am trusting in you, O Lord, saying, 'You are my God!'
My future is in your hands" (Psalm 31:14-15).

Some Key Words to Consider

The first two key words of our *Reset* that I want to highlight are *begin* and *end*. It should be obvious that the way we begin and end each day is important. Let me give you a common example. If you are a parent, you have probably had the experience of trying to help a fussy child, who "got up on the wrong side of the bed," to start his or her day. Not only did that fussy child probably ruin his or her own morning, but usually the atmosphere for the whole family as well. On the other end of the day, every parent has experienced many challenging nights where the bedtime routine evolved into a world war of major proportions. Children seem to enjoy pulling both Mom and Dad into a thirty-minute tag-team effort to get them to go to sleep!

That reminds me of a funny story. When our twin boys were young toddlers, I developed a great routine for getting them to go to sleep at night. We had their room arranged with two crib beds set up on opposite walls. There was about five feet of carpeted floor space that separated the two cribs. I had purchased a soothing sixty-minute cassette tape that played little short nursery rhyme songs, along with some basic sections devoted to beginning counting and the letters of the alphabet. I figured that it would help them to go to sleep and help them get a head start in their preschool education. But wait, there's more. (Sorry, I know that sounded like a TV infomercial!)

In the background of the tape was the sound of a heartbeat, something that resembled the sound of a mother's heartbeat in the womb. The first few nights it worked miracles! I would lie on the floor in the darkened room to enforce the "quiet-time, go-to-sleep rule." Within minutes of soft relaxing music, some slow-paced counting, sleepy repetitions of the alphabet, and the sound of somebody else's rhythmic heartbeat, Jonathan and Jeremiah were sound asleep. I would then get up off the floor and quietly slip out to brag to my wife how easy it was!

However, my string of successful bedtime duty nights was unfortunately broken on the fifth night before I could set any new parenting records. My wife swung open the boys' bedroom door when they started getting louder and louder, jumping up and down and laughing at each other, and obviously not going down as quickly as usual. What was worse was the sound of loud snoring that I was belching out from the carpeted floor in sync with the make-believe heartbeats on the cassette tape. I told you it was a soothing and relaxing tape! Do you know that I still have that cassette tape in one of our memory boxes up in our attic? I can't wait to try it out one day on some future grandkids and show their parents that I still have a secret touch for getting kids to go to sleep at night. The next time though, I will set a vibrating alarm on my cell phone for ten or fifteen minutes to make sure I don't get caught falling asleep again.

Oh yes, I was sharing about the importance of how we begin and end of each day. The way that children begin and end their days has great potential to unravel even the most patient mom or dad. Most parents know what I am talking about and know that those brief few moments at the beginning and end of each day can make or break a whole day for everyone. That is why parents are wise to teach children the importance of making those moments of the day peaceful ones, as much as possible.

God, our heavenly Father, tries to teach us the same thing about the beginning and end of our days, especially when it comes to our trust in Him. When we get up to begin each day, it is the starting point for that day and for the next twenty-four hour portion of our journey. We embark on the day with our first steps on the floor. Before we even place our second foot down, we should already be trusting God wholeheartedly with His plans for that day. Likewise, when we end our day, when our nightly routine serves to close the books on that day's events, we should be already be trusting God wholeheartedly with His plans for tomorrow's portion of the journey.

Another key word to understand is *trust*. Even though other people may have betrayed your trust sometime in your past, God wants you to still trust Him. That means that you can fully rely on Him. You can put your complete confidence in Him and in His unchanging character. You can definitely depend on Him according to His Word. Trusting God means that you are placing yourself and your future in His hands. In the palm of His hands, He will work all things in your life together for good. He is the master potter in the Old Testament book of Jeremiah, and your life is the moldable clay in His hands. Will you trust your life in His capable hands? With that picture fresh in your mind, read again our verse from Psalm 31:14-15.

"I am trusting in you, O Lord, saying, 'You are my God!'
My future is in your hands" (Psalm 31:14-15).

Review

Reset #_____

I _____ and _____ each day trusting God _____ with his plans for my _____.

"I am t_____ you, O Lord, saying, 'You are my _____!' My future is in your h_____" Psalm 31:14–15.

Review this last *Reset* several times today. Say it aloud to yourself, focusing on the importance of each word. Begin picturing your life and your future in the palm of God's hand as He works all things together for your good!

Review each of the previous six *Reset* cards at least once. See if you can say them in sequence, limiting your glances at your cards. Also continue reading aloud the verses and memorizing them as well.

Today's Prayer

O God,

You are my God! Furthermore, you are the potter and I am the clay! Help me to learn to trust you more today. I want to begin and end each day wholeheartedly trusting you and your plans for my future. Thank you for wanting to heal my past hurts and disappointments in life. I no longer need to let them weigh me down with unnecessary fear of ever trusting anyone again. I will start today by placing my life and my trust in you. Amen.

Day 26

Let's Play Jeopardy!
Who Said That? . . . for $1,000

Since it first aired on television back in 1964, millions of people have enjoyed watching the question and answer game show, *Jeopardy*. In fact, my wife's dad and mom had a nightly routine of sitting in their recliners and watching *Wheel of Fortune* and *Jeopardy* after their local news, and then it would be close to their bedtime around 8:00 p.m. That would be early for most of us to call it a day, but all the grandkids knew that Grandpa Murphy would be up early the next morning to read his Bible and have his personal devotion time. By the time the sun was creeping up over the horizon, he was usually out the door and off to tend to his large garden during the growing season.

He died in October 2010, just sixteen days after the family and his church had put together a surprise birthday party to help him celebrate his ninetieth birthday! Grandpa Murphy loved his ice cream, and in the pictures from that celebration, he has the biggest smile on his face as he scooped his own ice cream to go with his birthday cake. He was so happy that day, and I'm glad we had that last party to make his day extra special. We all miss him dearly and at his funeral, I spoke a few words about his strong legacy of daily reading the Bible and his exemplarily devotion to prayer. He was quite a godly man who all the grandkids and great-grandkids will remember for a long time.

There is another reason why I referred to *Jeopardy* in the title to this chapter. As I was trying to be creative in introducing what I want to emphasize today, I kept thinking about well-known statements and quotes that stand the test of time and live on long after the person who said them dies. I have even used a few quotes in other places in this book to make a point. In a few moments, I want to give you a quote and let you pretend that it is your turn as a contestant on *Jeopardy*, and you have just chosen your next category, "Who Said That?" for $1,000.

However, I cannot resist the temptation to divert for a moment to share a few of my favorite dry-humor quotes from one of the greatest deliverer of funny one-liners ever, Yogi Berra, the legendary New York Yankees catcher. These would be easy to recognize if they ever appeared in a "Who Said That?" category. Let me share a few of my favorite "Yogi-isms" for you to enjoy.

1. Never answer an anonymous letter.
2. A nickel ain't worth a dime anymore.
3. The future ain't what it used to be.
4. Half of the lies they tell about me aren't true.
5. Baseball is 90 percent mental—the other half is physical.
6. If you don't know where you are going, chances are you will end up somewhere else.
7. You should always go to other people's funerals; otherwise, they won't come to yours.
8. You better cut the pizza in four pieces because I'm not hungry enough to eat six.
9. Ninety percent of the putts that are short don't go in.
10. (This is one of my favorites!) Once, Yogi's wife, Carmen, asked, "Yogi, you are from St. Louis; we live in New Jersey, and you play ball in New York. If you go before I do, where would you like me to have you buried?" Yogi replied, "Surprise me."

See If You Know Who Said This!

Back now to our imaginary *Jeopardy* game, and you have just selected "Who Said That?" for $1000. The following answer is revealed: "I want your will to be done, not mine." Could you quickly formulate the correct answer to that quotation in a question-form before the other contestants? Do you know who said it? If you are thinking Jesus, congratulations, you are correct.

In Matthew 26:39, we find the context of that statement. Jesus is in the Garden of Gethsemane with Peter, James, and John. Matthew writes, "He went on a little farther and bowed with his face to the ground, praying, 'My Father! If it is possible, let this cup of suffering be taken away from me. Yet I want your will to be done, not mine.'"

In another passage in John's gospel, Jesus says something similar. "For I have come down from heaven to do the will of God who sent me, *not* to do my own will" (John 6:38, emphasis added).

In this 28-day *reset* journey, part of the transformation in our thinking has been to learn to walk daily in God's presence, to navigate each day's journey making our choices, while considering that God's way is always best. Now in this last *Reset*, we continue by wholeheartedly trusting God with His plans for our futures. In the Bible, we are encouraged to imitate the life of Jesus. So let us think about that for a moment.

In the first quote above, Jesus was praying to God before His impending crucifixion, and implied from His prayer, we know that He was completely yielded to His Father's plan for His future. While He agonized over the terrible magnitude of His mission to go to the cross, He knew that it was God's way for Him to pay the ultimate price for the sins of the world. From the second quote above, we can conclude that Jesus had understood this commitment from the earliest days of His public ministry. His focus was to always go about doing the will of His heavenly Father. In fact, it appears that every time He was around individuals or great crowds of people and witnessed their cares and hurts and diseases, He responded and adjusted His daily agenda to do the will of God who had sent Him.

If we are to follow the example of Jesus, then is it not important for us to recognize that Jesus's purpose was not about accomplishing His plans, but it was always about fulfilling God's plan for His life? If that is true, then when we begin and end each day by trusting God wholeheartedly with His plans for our futures, then we should do like Jesus and yield our plans to the plans of God. This is by no means an easy thing for us modern-day believers to do. Our cultures and lifestyles teach us to rely so much on self-determination and to aggressively mapping out our own life plans. Do not take me wrong.

Not all life planning is bad. In fact, many good Christian books even guide and help us do appropriate life mapping.

On the other hand, in this *reset* journey, I just want us to remember the sovereignty of our God and realize that when we can only partially see the road ahead, He can always see it all. Furthermore, He knows what is absolutely best for us. You and I can and should wisely consider the paths that we choose to take in life. We must also carefully weigh out all the options when we have choices to make. Our best decision-making efforts will be required for major choices in life, such as what careers to pursue, whom to marry, and where to live. Of course, we will make some mistakes along the way.

However, if you diligently guard your heart and thereby enable yourself to walk daily in God's presence, then don't you think that your chances of making better choices and fulfilling God's plan for your life will be much improved? Many of us have wasted years chasing some foggy self-notions of what we thought our lives should be. We have chased dream after dream only to feel let down when we actually achieved some of them. Could it be possible that God's plans would have been even better that ours?

Psalm 57: 2 is a great verse that says, "I cry out to God Most High, to God who will fulfill his purpose for me." Now that is a promise that most of us would be wise to reflect on and to pray for earnestly as we begin and end each day trusting God. Not only can we trust God, but we also know that He has a plan or a purpose for us that He promises to fulfill in our lives.

Now you may be knowledgeable when it comes to game shows and would know many answers to a "Who Said That?" category. While Yogi Berra's quotes are funny and thought provoking, I think that Jesus's quote, "I want your will to be done, not mine," is easily the one we need to give serious thought to modeling our life after. What do you think?

Review

Hopefully, you have mastered most of the earlier *Reset* statements. Here you will see each of the seven *Resets* started. Try to complete each one and only refer to your cards as needed. Later, review the verses for each one.

1. I am on God's mind . . .
2. I believe that God exists . . .
3. I now visualize God bending . . .
4. I receive and embrace Jesus . . .
5. I diligently guard my heart . . .
6. I will navigate life's journey . . .
7. I begin and end each day . . .

Today's Prayer

Dear God,

I am amazed at how clearly your Word speaks to every generation of people. While many people today discredit and dismiss the Bible as just an irrelevant, ancient holy text and out-of-date for modern humanity, I believe that its truths are eternal and changeless. It is relevant and timely for all generations, and it stands firm in heaven! What it says is reliable and true for me, and I receive it as your source of authority to me directly. As I walk with you daily, you are always showing me your will and teaching me what way is best for my life. Today, Lord, I ask you to fulfill your purpose for my life as I trust in you wholeheartedly. Help me to learn to yield my agenda to your agenda. You are my God! My hope and my future are secure in your hands. Amen.

Day 27

Where Is All This Hope Coming From?

If you were searching the Bible to find something good about the topic of love, you would probably start at 1 Corinthians 13, commonly known as the "Love Chapter." It is a great chapter on love's noble and lofty characteristics. However, overlooked in the last verse of that same chapter is something that we need to refer to today as we explore and excavate the topic of hope. Verse 13 says, "Three things will last forever—faith, hope, and love—and the greatest of these is love."

Extract the word *hope* out, and let's just focus on it today. Notice that the first part of the verse declares that along with faith and love, hope will last forever! That is awesome news in a world where it is easy to lose our hope. Think about how many times we hear the word *hopeless* used in our world each day. Just watch the nightly news (maybe that might not be such a good idea!). There are hopeless conflicts streaming to us live from all around the world. There is hopeless economic news reported to us almost every day. Our national debt is growing hopelessly out of control. Ravaging fires are hopelessly destroying thousands of acres of forest and the homes of families lying in their path. The hopeless images of floods and earthquakes propel the devastation right into our living rooms. In many cities, school districts struggle to find answers to the hopeless situations they face with falling student performances, hindered by under-budgeting or improper leadership and vision. Closer to home, most families today find themselves in hopeless situations with lost jobs and income, the lack of security in the jobs they have, the rising costs of living, heavy pressures of too much debt, and on and on the list could go.

All of us have experienced that feeling of hopelessness. You may even be going through a season of it right now. That is why I am so eager to give you the last portion of *Reset #7* today. Add the following statement to your index card now and then we will explore its potential to change your life dramatically!

God is my source again today of overflowing confident hope.

Do You Know What You Can't Live Without?

It is funny what people will say sometimes, especially when they say something and use the over-exaggerated phrase, "I think I will just die." Girls might say, "I'll just die if my boyfriend doesn't call me this weekend!" Boys might say, "I'll just die if she turns me down when I ask her for a date." Adults might say, "I'll just die if I don't get that promotion at work."

The following numbers will vary depending on which medical report you read and other various individual physical characteristics, but there could be general agreement with this summary.

A person can live without food for about *four* weeks.
A person can live without water for about *four* days.
A person can live without oxygen for about *four* minutes.
But a person cannot live without hope for *one second*.

God designed us physically to need regular amounts of food, water, and oxygen. Yes, we can live without them for a while, but soon we will begin feeling the effects of living without them. Hope, on the other hand, seems to be something that we need a consistent supply of in order to live up to our fullest potential. Think about it. When hope is depleted in your life, your joy and energy begins to evaporate quickly, bringing on that sickening feeling in the pit of your stomach. All of us know that terrible feeling too well.

It is funny how often we will declare things to be hopeless, which indicates what we are really saying is that our hope has run out. We are on empty. There is nothing left in our hope tanks. *Do you know that God does not ever want you to have an empty hope tank?* So why do we live so much of our lives acting as if hope has such a limited supply?

The truth is that living with hope is how we best live. Hope is what gets us from day to day, from week to week, and from year to year. Reality tells us that life is hard and that we will suffer some losses along the way. We can sustain many of those losses for a while, but without a steady stream of overflowing and confidence-building hope, we will eventually deplete most of our innate energy and ability to fight on. That is when we will be tempted to throw in the towel and simply give up.

A Prayer That Will Fill You Up With Overflowing Confident Hope

The New Testament book of Romans is a fascinating book to read and gives us a great vision of the Apostle Paul's insight into the plans and purposes of God for his people. Near the end of this letter to the believers and followers of Christ in Rome, Paul injects a two-sentence life changing prayer that should forever dispel our notions of true hopelessness. This verse is found in Romans 15:13 and becomes our second supportive verse for *Reset* #7. You will want to add this to the back of your *Reset* card.

> "I pray that God, the source of hope, will fill you completely with joy and peace because you trust in him. Then you will overflow with confident hope through the power of the Holy Spirit" (Romans 15:13).

In our human ways of thinking, we think that hope has a limited shelf life. However, remember when we mentioned at the beginning of this chapter that hope lasts forever? It cannot be both ways, so which way is it? I think it is now obvious, especially since Paul also reminds us in his prayer that the source of hope is God himself. Since God is eternal, does it not make sense that He could also be the eternal source of an ever flowing and overflowing river of hope?

Furthermore, Paul describes the projected outcome or net result of jumping into the everlasting supply of God's hope with the word *overflow*. Just think about it. *God Himself is the eternal source, the origin, the wellspring, and the fountain of this never-ending supply of hope.* In addition, He will also fill you completely with real joy and peace, which will come into your life concurrently on the heels of hope. By choosing to live each day in the steady stream of overflowing confident hope through the indwelling of the Holy Spirit, you should never again have to experience an empty hope tank!

In my earlier years, my hope tank sometimes got close to empty. Most of the time though, I found myself living somewhere near the half-full or half-empty mark, depending on whether I was feeling either optimistic or pessimistic. Notice that I used the word *feeling*. We should never base our hope on how we feel. Hope is based solely on eternal facts. It took me a while to learn that truth, but now I know, and so do you. Hope is based on God, who is the source of our everlasting confident hope.

Three Pegs to Hang Your Hope On

Since eternal truth and fact are much better anchoring pegs than temporary feelings to hang your hope on, let me give you three pegs that will put this whole issue of hope into proper perspective.

1. Jesus is alive and in heaven right now.
2. Jesus is preparing your place in heaven right now.
3. Jesus has your eternal destiny is his hands right now.

From now on, do not ever again think that hope has a short shelf life or that you can base your hope on feelings. Rather, know the facts concerning hope. God is the source of your hope. That hope is constantly flowing like a mighty river, and it is consistent with God's plans and purpose for your life. If you have embraced and received Jesus as your personal Savior, He has secured your salvation and your future by His life, death, and resurrection. He is alive in heaven right now, preparing a place for you. Your eternity has already been determined.

Knowledge of these truths will help you to stand strong, even on your toughest days. With all this settled as factual, you should not have to stay stuck living as you were before you embarked on this *reset* journey. God never engineered your hope tank to be empty or even half-full. Instead, He intends for you to max out and overflow with hope so that some of His hope will spill out on others around you. So from now on, in spite of what the current circumstances in your life are, you should take your first step each day with a sense of overflowing confident hope.

Let this be a gentle reminder. You can have this kind of hope and yet still have to face tough trials at the same time. Those are the days when you will really need to pray and ask God for his help and guidance to allow eternal hope to win the battles over despair. To help you during those times, here is a helpful acrostic using the letters *H-O-P-E.*

Holding
On
Praying
Expectantly

Review

We have finished the seventh and last *Reset* today. See if you can fill in the blanks below. Then review it by reading it aloud to yourself. Learn it well enough so that you can say it tonight as your last thought before you go to sleep.

Reset # _____

I _____ ____ _____ each day _____ God wholeheartedly with his _____ for my _____.

God is my _____ again today of _____ _____ hope.

"I am _____ you, O Lord, saying, 'You ____ __ ____!' My _____ is in your _____" Psalm 31:14–15.

"I pray that God, the _____ of _____, will fill you completely with joy and peace because you _____ in him. Then you will overflow with _____ hope through the power of the Holy Spirit" Romans 15:13.

Today's Prayer

O God, my source of overflowing confident hope!

Thank you for the facts about Jesus that give me strong pegs to hang my hope on. Let me echo Paul's prayer in my own life that I might be filled with an overflowing confident hope that leads to real peace and joy. Even though I can do without food and water for a little while, Lord, I cannot live without hope. You are my source again today of overflowing confident hope and my future is in your strong hands. Amen.

Day 28

Continuing the Journey . . .
"I Am Now in It to Win It!"

Congratulations! Today you are going to conclude this 28-day book journey, and the title to this last chapter is like a bonus *Reset* statement for you to internalize. "I am now in it to win it!" You might even want to use it as the theme to your own personal daily "one shining moment" mental video. Back on Day 1, we imagined how nice it would be to play back such a highlight video in your mind each evening! You may recognize part of this phrase, "in it to win it," because it has become a popular phrase of American Idol judge, Randy Jackson, when he is giving his thumbs-up encouraging approval to one of the singing contestants. This past television season, Randy would often end his critic of a singer's performance by declaring something like, "America, I'm telling you, (so and so) is rocking it again tonight and (he or she) is in it to win it!"

Although this completes your 28-day *reset* journey with me, you are now also in it to win it. For you, today is the end of reading a book, but it is just the beginning of an even greater lifetime walk with God. Each day, our purpose has been to help you *reset* your life and start enjoying a genuine daily relationship with Him. As I stated a few days ago, I was beginning to regret our fast-approaching last day together, but that was only because on a human level, we will lose the daily contact that we have enjoyed through the days spent together in this book. However, I believe that in some way, as you continue to review and daily use these seven *Resets* and verses in your life, we will all be seeking and following the same God and continue being part of the spiritual family that He is building up all around the world. A book by its nature has to end, and we may just have to imagine shaking hands or hugging each other as new friends getting ready to depart for now on our separate ways. Yet, one day we will meet again either somewhere here on earth or in heaven, or maybe even in another book.

The Goal and a Brief Summary of *The Reset*

Here is my simple goal for *The Reset*. I desperately want you and many others of all ages and from all walks of life to reclaim and live the lives that God wants for you and that is pleasing to Him. You live in a world that is full of powerful factors and influences that will constantly try to pull you away from God. The things that are ungodly and sinful will separate you from God, and if that happens, the very life that is God's best for you will soon be a fading image in your rearview mirror. The good news is that you have the choice every day to either come to God or to walk away from Him. No matter what your life was like prior to starting this 28-day journey, God has never given up on you. You really do matter to Him. He thinks precious thoughts about you all the time. It does not even matter what other people have said about you and how much of that you have believed up to this point in your life. You may even have gone through some terribly devastating events in your life and often felt like your hope tank was empty. However, God's truth prevails over your feelings every time!

The truth is that you are still on God's mind today, even if you have just messed up again, maybe for the umpteenth time. But God's unchanging character stands on His love and His great faithfulness, even in the dark shadows of our sin and unfaithfulness. He will always have good thoughts about you. He unconditionally loves you and desperately wants you to come back to Him. That is great news for you at this potential turning point in your life, and you should respond to Him by letting God be on your mind too. All you must do is believe that He exists and that what He says to you through His Word is authoritatively reliable and true. Start praying and talking to God and visualize Him in your mind bending down to hear and answer you when you pray, and ask Him for His help and guidance.

If you have never received and embraced Jesus as your personal Savior, just do it! You will immediately become a friend of God and begin to enjoy a new relationship of being made right with Him forever. All of your past mistakes and sins will be forgiven. You must start now to diligently guard your heart every day. Satan will constantly try to sabotage and steal, kill, and destroy your new relationship with God. Therefore, be victorious in the battle by always keeping your heart ready to receive God's overflowing grace and mercy. A guarded heart that is kept clean or pure determines the moment-by-moment course of your life, and it will enable you to rest peacefully in God's goodness and to walk daily in His presence. Practice and learn how to navigate your life's journey and make your daily choices, keeping in mind that God's way is always going to be the best for you.

Finally, begin and end each day from now on choosing to trust God wholeheartedly with His plans for your future. If you develop this kind of relationship with God, then He will be your daily source of overflowing, confident hope. Life will still have its difficult places and trials to navigate through, but "you will be in it to win it" through the power of the Holy Spirit.

Romans 12:2 was your launching verse for this *reset* journey. Now read the complete verse and let its full context seal your commitment to continue the *reset* journey in your life. My emphasis is added in italics here.

"Don't copy the behavior and customs of this world, but *let God transform you into a new person by changing the way you think.* Then you will learn to know God's will for you, which is good and pleasing and perfect."

So What Will *The Reset* Lead to in Your Life?

That is a good question. I do not have the answers for your life in particular, but God does, and I do know that He wants to fulfill His plans and purposes in your life. He also wants you to have a dream for your life. Psalm 37:4 says, "Take delight in the Lord, and he will give you your heart's desires." Maybe your life has had some hard places that took some of the desires and dreams right out of your heart. Maybe somewhere along the way, you gave up on yourself and allowed your desires to slip right out of your hands. You are now at a crucial turning point in your life. However, it is always too early to quit!

That reminds me of a little story where a father once said to his boy,

"Son, you gotta set a goal and never quit. Remember George Washington?"
The son said, "Yes."
"Remember Thomas Jefferson?"
Again, the son said, "Yes."
"Do you remember Abraham Lincoln?"
"Why, of course, Dad. I remember Lincoln!"
The father said, "They didn't quit! Do you remember Ozador McIngle?"
The son quickly responded, "No, who was he?"
The father shot back, "See there, you don't remember him. He quit!"

Even though I may not know you personally, I do know that you have what I call *undeserved significance* in God's eyes. He is always thinking precious thoughts about you and has created you with a unique plan or purpose for your life. Keep asking and seeking God until He shows you what He wants you to do. You really do matter to God! In recent days or years, you may have experienced some rough seas that have weakened your resolve to keep on keeping on. But God is the God of new beginnings, new hopes, new strengths, new visions, new encouragements, new powers, new determinations, new chances, and a new life! At this point, I urge you to let God and *The Reset* give you a fresh start. You can be set free from your past and begin to dream and hope again for a bright future, walking with God and overflowing with a confident hope that comes from him!

My message to you is to give God a chance. Listen to Him. Allow Him to guide you to a better place. Find out what the dreams and desires are that He wants you to pursue at this stage of your life. Then pursue them! Give them everything that you have. Let them become the takeoff points for your "one shining moment!" Tell yourself, "I am now in it to win it!"

For some reason, I have always had this dream to help and encourage others to pursue God's best for them and to reach for the sky and make a difference in their world. For many years, I fulfilled this desire by challenging children to believe that God's way would always be best in their lives. Now, my desire and dream is that, with God's help, *The Reset* will multiply the potential for me to do the same with even more people. Will you now be the next one to internalize the seven *Reset* statements and utilize them to reclaim God's way in your life?

A Final Example of How One Life Was *Reset* to Fulfill a Desire

In March 2005, I was leaving a former place of ministry where I had helped establish a vibrant and visionary ministry to children, from infants through sixth grade. I had a wonderful and fabulous team of ministry leaders and class pastors there that made my time at that church so much fun and fulfilling. While the children's ministry was changing the lives of many children, many parents and other adults were also discovering their own strategic places in the plans and purposes of God for these children. On my last Sunday at the church, it was an emotional time for my family and me as we trusted God and began our transition into another season of our lives.

A few days later, I got an e-mail from Connie, a dear woman who put into perspective for me how her thinking had changed in her decision to volunteer in our preschool department. Anyone who has ever tried to recruit volunteers for a preschool department knows the never-ending challenge to have enough volunteers. A few years earlier, I had such an immediate need for some preschool volunteers that I asked for permission to give a short recruitment invitation in one of our older adult classes for new volunteers to step up and teach in our preschool department. The mostly blank and expressionless stares told me that I was probably not going to fill any of my empty slots that day. However, Connie called me later that week and wanted to help if she could. Soon, Connie jumped in with such enthusiasm and became one of my best preschool class pastors (we asked our volunteers to be like a pastor to their children and their parents, not just teachers). Now, let me paraphrase and share with you portions of her e-mail that she sent to me several years later as my wife and I were leaving to pursue another career.

Dear Pastor David,

It has been an emotional day for me with your announcement to leave us. I have grown to love and respect you for your leadership these past few years and feel very sad to see you leave, but I pray that God will continue to bless you as you and Pam move on to newer things.

I have gone to church all my life and have been a Christian since I was eight years old, even though I was not baptized until much later in life. I accepted Jesus as my Lord and Savior when I was young, and my mother refused to let me get baptized. She thought that my grandmother had coerced me to go forward. Anyway, the reason I tell you this is that I have attended church for many years, but it wasn't until you came to our class and told us about the need for a Bumblebee Class Pastor that I actually felt God speak directly to me in my heart. Because of you and you only, I have been able to realize the best blessings these last three years by ministering to those little children. I receive as much or more from them each Sunday than they are ever receiving from me! Hearing them recite their Bible verses and recalling the last week's lesson is a precious gift to me from God every week. I thank you for taking the time to guide and help me become the person that makes a difference in their lives by making a difference in my life too.

I once read in a book that when we get to heaven, there will be a time when every person that we have shared Jesus with and have helped along the way will be shown to us. You, my friend will be tired of standing by the time Jesus gets through showing you the people that you have influenced. I pray that by the time I get to heaven, my legs will be tired too!

I wish you and Pam many blessings and much happiness.

Your sister in Christ . . . Connie.

The Wrap-Up

My friend, thanks for sharing this *reset* journey with me. Continue reviewing the seven *Resets* and verses until you know them well. Use them constantly as you let God transform you into a new person by changing the way you think. With seven days in a week, you might try focusing on a different *Reset* each day of the week for variety. Learn them and say them to yourself often. Try praying the *Reset* statements as I have often done throughout our journey. Of course, find other ways to grow in your walk with God. Find a good Bible-teaching church to get involved with regularly. Read your Bible and other good books that will help you grow spiritually. Spend time with God each day and pray. When difficulties come your way, remember the hope acrostic, **H**ang **O**n **P**raying **E**xpectantly! Be an encourager to others and use your opportunities to share *The Reset* and give someone else a fresh start in his or her life. I would love to hear from you if you ever have a personal "one shining moment" replay that you would like to share, or even relay the *reset* story of another person whose life you have made a difference in.

Let me give you one final thought as you continue the journey and implement the seven *Resets* to reclaim your rightful relationship with God.

> *No matter what kind of start you had,*
> *you can now have a great finish!*

So, until we meet again . . . somewhere . . . someday . . .
Go and reclaim the life you should be living!

You can contact me at:
the28dayRESET@gmail.com

NOTES

Day 1 Introduction: "One Shining Moment, You Reached for the Sky!"
1. "One Shining Moment," words and music by David Barrett Hodges Song Supply/ASCAP, http://www.oneshiningmoment. com/lyrics/index.html (May 25, 2011). Used by permission.

Day 2: A Fresh Start Would Be Nice
1. Shad Helmstetter, adapted from *What to Say When You Talk to Yourself.* (New York: Pocket Books, 1982), 70-71.

Day 3: You Are on God's Mind Again Today
1. Zig Ziglar, *Raising Positive Kids in a Negative World* (Nashville: Oliver-Nelson Books, 1985), 79.

Day 4: Changing How You See Yourself
1. Bill Glass, adapted from *Expect to Win* (Waco: Word, Inc., 1981), 110-111.

Day 5: We All Love Rescue Stories
1. Wayne Jacobsen, *He Loves Me!* (Newberry Park: Windblown Media, 2007), 31.

Day 7: It's Time to Take a Stand
1. F.F. Bruce, *The Epistle to the Hebrews* (Grand Rapids: Wm. B. Eerdmans Publishing Company, 1964), 290.

Day 10: We All Need Some Help Getting Around in Life

1. Ron Mehl, *God Works the Night Shift* (Sisters: Multnomah Books, 1994), 63.

2. Mehl, 56-57. Used by permission of Compassion Ministries, P.O. Box 91516, Portland, Oregon, 97291.

Day 11: God's Arms Are Never Folded When We Go to Him

1. Ron Mehl, *God Works the Night Shift* (Sisters: Multnomah Books, 1994), 148-149. Used by permission of Compassion Ministries, P.O. Box 91516, Portland, Oregon, 97291.

Day 14: The Ultimate Reset

1. Dare 2 Share Ministries, http://www.dare2share.org/resources/ free/ "Gospel Journey" (July, 2011)

2. Andy Stanley, *How Good Is Good Enough* (Sisters: Multnomah Publishers, Inc., 2003), 90.

Day 21: A Trail Guide Who Knows the Way Ahead

1. Henry T. Blackaby and Richard Blackaby. *Experiencing God Day-By-Day* (Nashville: B&H Publishing Group, 1998), 122.

Day 22: What Will You Decide to Do Next?

1. Shad Helmstetter, *What to Say When You Talk to Yourself* (New York: Pocket Books, 1982), 251.

RESET STATEMENTS	BIBLE VERSES (NLT)
1. I am on God's mind again today. (even if I just messed up.) I really do matter to God, and He is always thinking precious thoughts about me. Today, I will let God be on my mind too.	Let God transform you into a new person by changing the way you think. Romans 12:2 How precious are your thoughts about me, O God. They cannot be numbered. Psalm 139:17
2. I believe that God exists, that His Word is true, and that real joy and strength are my rewards for seeking Him.	Anyone who wants to come to him must believe that God exists and that he rewards those who sincerely seek him. Hebrews 11:6 The joy of the Lord is your strength. Nehemiah 8:10
3. I now visualize God bending down to personally hear and answer me when I pray and ask for His help and guidance.	Bend down, O Lord, and hear my prayer; answer me, for I need your help. Psalm 86:1 O Lord, you are so good, so ready to forgive, so full of unfailing love for all who ask for your help. Psalm 86:5
4. I receive and embrace Jesus as my personal Savior, and I now enjoy my relationship of being made right with God forever. I am a friend of God based on grace and forgiveness.	Then I called on the name of the Lord: "Please, Lord, save me!" Psalm 116:4 Everyone who calls on the name of the Lord will be saved. Romans 10:13 If you confess with your mouth that Jesus is Lord and believe in your heart that God raised him from the dead, you will be saved. For it is by believing in your heart that you are made right with God, and it is by confessing with your mouth that you are saved. Romans 10:9-10

RESET STATEMENTS	BIBLE VERSES (NLT)
5. I diligently guard my heart to keep it ready to receive God's overflowing grace and mercy, which are brand new to me every single day. This enables me to rest peacefully in God's goodness and to walk daily in His presence.	Guard your heart above all else, for it determines the course of your life. Proverbs 4:23 Let my soul be at rest again, for the Lord has been good to me. Psalm 116:7 I walk in the Lord's presence as I live here on the earth! Psalm 116:9
6. I will navigate life's journey today and make my daily choices knowing that God's way is always best.	"I am the Lord your God, who teaches you what is good for you and leads you along the paths you should follow." Isaiah 48:17
7. I begin and end each day trusting God wholeheartedly with His plans for my future. God is my source again today of overflowing confident hope.	I am trusting you, O Lord, saying, "You are my God!" My future is in your hands. Psalm 31:14-15 I pray that God, the source of hope, will fill you completely with joy and peace because you trust in him. Then you will overflow with confident hope through the power of the Holy Spirit. Romans 15:13

CPSIA information can be obtained at www.ICGtesting.com
Printed in the USA
LVOW071714181111

255270LV00005B/9/P